Special Day COOKING

A Life Skills Cookbook

Beverly Worth Palomba

Special Day Publishing
San Francisco

Published by Special Day Publishing
San Francisco, CA
www.specialdaycooking.com

ISBN: 978-0-9897082-0-3

Library of Congress Control Number: 2013912757

Design: Marcy Claman

First printing
Printed in China

Callawind
Custom Cookbooks

Produced by Callawind Custom Cookbooks
(a division of Callawind Publications Inc.)
www.callawind.com

Special Day Cooking

Dear Chefs,

Cooking and sharing a recipe is fun and exciting . . .

And it is time for a cookbook especially for you!

Cooking is a life skill that is used every day from the simplest form of making a peanut butter and jelly sandwich to baking a pie, preparing your own lunch to helping prepare dinner, or serving a snack for friends to bringing a dessert to a party. It is entertaining! You feel wonderful about yourself and it is exciting to see the smiles on your family and friends' faces when you cook something special for them.

Cooking is a skill and just like any other skill (computer, gymnastics, or bowling), it can be learned with practice. And what fun the practicing is!! Like other skills, cooking can be an exciting activity to do with others. But remember to giggle when something goes wrong because it happens to everyone. Be patient with yourself and have a good time.

I wrote the recipes in large type, and formatted them in consistent, easy to follow steps. There are beginning recipes to start with and more involved recipes once you have learned the cooking process and are ready to move on. Once you are familiar with a recipe it shouldn't take more than about 1 hour to make.

I hope you enjoy cooking and eating your creations as much as the young people I have taught over the years. We have had many joyful hours together being creative and socializing all while building our self-confidence and self-esteem.

Enjoy!!
Chef Beverly

~ TABLE OF CONTENTS ~

~ HELPFUL HINTS ~

Cutting:
For safety reasons, use a plastic knife when cutting. To help you remember not to push when cutting: sing-song; "saw, saw, saw".

Cutting Boards:
A cutting board with a rubber backing will stop the cutting board from slipping on your working surface.

Cracking an Egg:
Crack your eggs into a small bowl before adding them to a recipe. It will be easier to remove any egg shell pieces that may have fallen in.

Dry Measuring Cups:
Metal dry measuring cups with long handles, with clearly marked measurements are best. They last longer, are easier to use, and the measurements won't wash off.

Following Directions:
Use a sticky arrow to follow the directions on your recipe. Put a sticky arrow next to the direction you are working on. Then move it to the next direction as you continue to work.

Large, Heavy Containers:
To make it easier to lift and pour from large containers, store your ingredients in smaller, lighter containers. This will make it easier to lift and pour from. For example; you can store vegetable oil in an empty spice jar or pour milk into a quart container.

Measuring and Storing Dry Ingredients:
To make it easier to scoop and level your dry ingredients, store your dry ingredients in wide, covered containers.

Measuring Liquid Ingredients:
Avoid spills by measuring small amounts of liquid ingredients over a small bowl.

Measuring Spoons:
Metal measuring spoons with clearly marked measurements that include a ⅛ measuring spoon are best. They last longer and the measurements won't wash off.

Pasta Cooker:
This is a product made from plastic for cooking pasta in the microwave. It is safer and easier to use than boiling water on the stove. The handles don't get very hot and you can cook, strain, and mix all in the same container. You can order these on-line.

Plastic Knife:
Be safe, use a plastic knife for cutting. All the recipes in this book requiring a knife for cutting can be done with a plastic knife. Also, you can use the back, straight side of the knife for leveling your ingredients.

~ PREPARING PLATE ~ PORTIONS

MyPlate.Gov

Myplate can help you make good food choices. Myplate is a new symbol and took the place of the Food Pyramid. It shows a plate with four parts indicating how much of each food group you should have at each meal. To the right of the plate is a blue circle. That circle is to remind you that some dairy should be part of every meal.

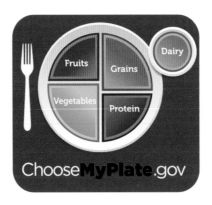

Fruits:

* You need 1½ cups of fruit each day.

* Have delicious, juicy fruit as a snack and with each meal.

* Some favorite fruits are: apples, cherries, strawberries, oranges, peaches, bananas, grapes and more . . .

Vegetables:

* You need 2½ cups of veggies each day.

* Crunchy vegetables is a delicious snack and important to have with your lunch and dinner.

* Some favorite vegetables are: tomatoes, potatoes, carrots, beans, peppers, peas, and more . . .

Grains:
* You need 6 ounces of grains each day.

* Have grains with each meal. One slice of bread, or a ½ cup of cooked oatmeal, rice, or pasta is only one serving.

* Some favorite grains are: bread, muffins, tortillas, crackers, cereal, oatmeal, pretzels, and more . . .

Protein:
* You need 5 ounces of protein each day.

* Include some protein with each meal.

* Some favorite protein foods are: low fat milk, cheese, beef, chicken, pork, eggs, fish, and more . . .

Dairy:
* You need 3 cups of dairy each day.

* Dairy is a great snack and important to have at each meal.

* Some favorite dairy foods are: low fat milk, cheese, yogurt, cottage cheese, and more . . .

Favorite
Breakfast
Recipes

A healthy breakfast is the most important meal of the day.
Kick off your day with energy!

FUN FACT   75 billion eggs are sold each year in the United States.

FUN FACT   There are more chickens than humans on earth.

~ BREAKFAST ~

A little more challenging

Breakfast Egg Muffin

Makes 1 Egg Muffin

Start your day the healthy way.

Gather Ingredients

* 1 egg

* ½ of a breakfast sausage patty
  Buy a package of fully cooked sausage.

* ½ tablespoon shredded Cheddar cheese

* 1 tablespoon salsa

* 1 tablespoon milk

* Salt and pepper shakers

* 1 English muffin

Gather Equipment

Put a paper towel on your cooking area to catch spills.

* Microwave and toaster

* 1 small microwave-safe bowl

* 1 cutting board

* Measuring spoons

* 1 small bowl Catch spills: measure over bowl.

* 1 plastic knife Be safe: cut with a plastic knife.

* 1 kitchen fork

* 1 kitchen teaspoon

* 2 pot holders

* 1 serving plate

Cooking Directions

Prepare Egg

1. **Crack** egg into small microwave-safe bowl.

2. **Cut** ½ breakfast sausage into small pieces on cutting board.
Be safe: cut sausage with a plastic knife.

3. **Add** sausage pieces to egg.

4. **Measure** ½ tablespoon shredded Cheddar cheese. **Add** to egg.

5. **Measure** 1 tablespoon salsa. Add to egg.

6. **Measure** 1 tablespoon milk. Add to egg.
Catch spills: measure milk over a small bowl, then add to egg.

7. **Add** 2 dashes of salt and pepper to egg.

8. **Mix** with kitchen fork. Set aside.

Cook English Muffin

1. **Split** English muffin in half. **Put** English muffin in toaster. **Push** toaster on.

Cook Egg *"while English muffin is cooking"*

1. **Microwave** egg 45 seconds. **Remove** bowl with pot holders.

2. **Mix** with kitchen fork.

3. **Microwave** egg again 45 seconds. **Remove** bowl with pot holders.

4. **Mix** with kitchen fork.

5. **Put** toasted English muffin on serving plate.

6. **Spoon** egg mixture on top of ½ of toasted English muffin.

7. **Put** 2nd half of English muffin on top of egg. **Eat** like a sandwich.

~ ENJOY!! ~

*When you finish cooking:
1. Put your ingredients and equipment away.
2. Wash and put your dishes away.
3. Wipe your cooking area clean.

13

Breakfast Smoothie

Makes 1 Smoothie

A refreshingly smooth breakfast!

Gather Ingredients

* ½ cup orange juice

* ¼ cup plain yogurt

* ½ banana

* 5 large strawberries

Gather Equipment

Put a paper towel on your cooking area to catch spills.

* Electric blender

* 1 cutting board

* ¼ dry measuring cup

* 1 liquid measuring cup

* 1 plastic knife
  Be safe: cut with a plastic knife.

* 1 kitchen teaspoon

* 1 serving glass

Cooking Directions

Make Smoothie

1. **Measure** ½ cup orange juice in liquid measuring cup. **Pour** into blender.

2. **Measure** ¼ cup yogurt in dry measuring cup. **Add** to blender.

3. **Peel** ½ banana. **Cut** into 2 pieces on cutting board. **Add** to blender.
Be safe: cut banana with a plastic knife.

4. **Put** 5 strawberries in your hand. **Rinse** under cold water in the sink.

5. **Cut** stems off strawberries on cutting board. **Cut** strawberries in half.
Be safe: cut strawberries with a plastic knife.

6. **Add** strawberries to blender.

Mix Smoothie

1. **Put** cover on blender.

2. **Keep** one hand on blender cover. **Mix** for 30 seconds. Count to 30.

3. **Pour** into serving glass.

~ ENJOY!! ~

✱ When you finish cooking:
1. Put your ingredients and equipment away.
2. Wash and put your dishes away.
3. Wipe your cooking area clean.

Cinnamon Toast

Makes 2 Pieces of Toast

Perfect with scrambled eggs or by itself.

Gather Ingredients

* 2 pieces of bread
* Butter or margarine for spreading
* Cinnamon/Sugar spice

Gather Equipment

Put a paper towel on your cooking area to catch spills.

* Toaster
* 1 kitchen knife
* 1 serving plate

Cooking Directions

Toast Bread

1. **Put** 2 pieces of bread into toaster. **Push** on.

2. **Put** toasted bread side-by-side on serving plate.

Make Cinnamon Toast

1. **Spread** butter over both pieces of toast with kitchen knife.

2. **Sprinkle** cinnamon/sugar spice over both pieces of toast.

3. **Cut** each piece of toast in half.

~ ENJOY!! ~

FUN FACT Cinnamon powder is ground up inner bark of the Cinnamon Tree.

* When you finish cooking:
1. Put your ingredients and equipment away.
2. Wash and put your dishes away.
3. Wipe your cooking area clean.

Crispy Bacon

Makes 3 Pieces

Fantastic with scrambled eggs.

Gather Equipment

Put a paper towel on your cooking area to catch spills.

* Microwave

* 2 paper towels

* 1 serving plate

Gather Ingredients

* 3 strips bacon
  Buy a package of fully cooked bacon.

Cooking Directions

Prepare Bacon

1. **Put** 2 paper towels on top of each other in the microwave.

2. **Lay** 3 bacon strips across paper towels.

Cook Bacon

1. **Microwave** bacon 1 minute.

2. **Put** bacon on serving plate.

~ ENJOY!! ~

FUN FACT Bacon Day is held on the Saturday before Labor Day.

*When you finish cooking:
1. Put your ingredients and equipment away.
2. Wash and put your dishes away.
3. Wipe your cooking area clean.

Easy Scrambled Eggs

Makes 1 Serving

Add bacon and cinnamon toast to complete this scrumptious breakfast.

Gather Ingredients

* 1 egg

* 1 tablespoon milk

* Salt and pepper shakers

Gather Equipment

Put a paper towel on your cooking area to catch spills.

* Microwave

* 1 small microwave-safe bowl

* Measuring spoons

* 1 small bowl
Catch spills: measure over bowl.

* 1 kitchen fork

* 1 kitchen teaspoon

* 2 pot holders

* 1 serving plate

Cooking Directions

Prepare Egg

1. **Crack** egg into small microwave-safe bowl.

2. **Measure** 1 tablespoon of milk. Add to egg.
   Catch spills: measure milk over a small bowl then add to egg.

3. **Add** 2 dashes of salt and pepper to egg.

4. **Mix** with kitchen fork.

Cook Egg

1. **Microwave** egg 30 seconds.

2. **Remove** bowl from microwave with pot holders. **Mix** with kitchen fork.

3. **Microwave** egg again 30 seconds.

4. **Remove** bowl from microwave with pot holders. **Mix** with kitchen fork.

5. **Spoon** onto serving plate.

~ ENJOY!! ~

* When you finish cooking:
1. Put your ingredients and equipment away.
2. Wash and put your dishes away.
3. Wipe your cooking area clean.

Fresh Strawberry Bagel

Makes 1 Bagel

Sweet, juicy strawberries, makes this breakfast special.

Gather Ingredients

* 2 fresh strawberries
* 1 plain bagel
* Plain cream cheese for spreading

Gather Equipment

Put a paper towel on your cooking area to catch spills.

* Toaster
* 1 plastic knife
  Be safe: use a plastic knife for cutting.
* 1 cutting board
* 1 serving plate

Cooking Directions

Prepare Strawberries

1. **Put** 2 strawberries in your hand. **Rinse** under cold water in the sink.

2. **Cut** stems off strawberries on cutting board.
   Be safe: cut strawberries with a plastic knife.

3. **Cut** strawberries into thin slices. **Set aside.**

Toast Bagel

1. **Cut** bagel in half on cutting board.
   Be safe: cut bagel with a plastic knife.

2. **Put** bagel in toaster. **Push** on.

3. **Put** toasted bagel slices side-by-side on serving plate.

Make Strawberry Bagel

1. **Spread** cream cheese over both halves of toasted bagel with plastic knife.

2. **Put** strawberry slices on top of cream cheese.

~ ENJOY!! ~

*When you finish cooking:
1. Put your ingredients and equipment away.
2. Wash and put your dishes away.
3. Wipe your cooking area clean.

Hot Cocoa

Makes 1 Cup

Perfect on a chilly day.

Gather Ingredients

* 3 tablespoons cocoa

* ¾ cup milk

* Mini marshmallows
  A small handful.

Gather Equipment

Put a paper towel on your cooking area to catch spills.

* Microwave

* 1 mug

* 1 liquid measuring cup

* Measuring spoons

* 1 kitchen teaspoon

* 2 pot holders

Cooking Directions

Heat Milk

1. **Measure** ¾ cup of milk in liquid measuring cup.

2. **Microwave** milk for 1 minute and 30 seconds.

3. **Remove** milk from microwave with pot holders. **Set aside.**

Make Cocoa

1. **Measure** 3 tablespoons of cocoa into mug.

2. **Pour** hot milk into mug.

3. **Mix** with kitchen teaspoon.

4. **Add** a small handful of mini marshmallows.

~ ENJOY!! ~

* When you finish cooking:
1. Put your ingredients and equipment away.
2. Wash and put your dishes away.
3. Wipe your cooking area clean.

Maple and Brown Sugar Oatmeal

Makes 1 Serving

Yummy sweet oatmeal.

Gather Ingredients

* ½ cup old-fashion oats

* ¾ cup water

* 2 teaspoons maple syrup

* 2 teaspoons brown sugar

* 1 tablespoon raisins

Gather Equipment

Put a paper towel on your cooking area to catch spills.

* Microwave

* 1 medium microwave-safe bowl

* 1 liquid measuring cup

* ½ dry measuring cup

* Measuring spoons

* 1 small bowl Catch spills: measure over bowl.

* 1 kitchen teaspoon

* 1 plastic knife Use knife to level ingredients.

* 2 pot holders

Cooking Directions

Make Oatmeal

1. **Measure** ½ cup old-fashioned oats in dry measuring cup.

2. **Pour** into medium microwave-safe bowl.

3. **Measure** ¾ cup water in liquid measuring cup. **Add** to oats.

4. **Mix** with kitchen teaspoon.

5. **Microwave** 90 seconds. **Remove** bowl from microwave with pot holders.

6. **Mix** with kitchen teaspoon.

Add Toppings

1. **Measure** 2 teaspoons maple syrup. **Add** to oats.
   Catch spills: measure maple syrup over small bowl, then add to oats.

2. **Measure** and **level** 2 teaspoons brown sugar. **Add** to oats.

3. **Measure** 1 tablespoon of raisins. **Add** to oats.

4. **Mix** with kitchen teaspoon.

5. **Microwave** 60 seconds. **Remove** bowl from microwave with pot holders.

6. **Mix** with kitchen teaspoon.

~ ENJOY!! ~

* When you finish cooking:
1. Put your ingredients and equipment away.
2. Wash and put your dishes away.
3. Wipe your cooking area clean.

Peanut Butter Banana Bagel

Makes 1 Bagel

Go Bananas!

Gather Equipment

Put a paper towel on your cooking area to catch spills.

* Toaster

* 1 cutting board

* 1 plastic knife
  Be safe: use a plastic knife for cutting.

* 1 serving plate

Gather Ingredients

* ½ banana

* 1 plain bagel

* Peanut butter for spreading

Cooking Directions

Prepare Banana

1. **Peel** ½ banana.

2. **Cut** 6 thin slices of banana on cutting board. **Set aside.**
   Be safe: cut banana with a plastic knife.

Toast Bagel

1. **Cut** bagel in half on cutting board.
   Be safe: cut bagel with a plastic knife.

2. **Put** bagel in toaster. **Push** on.

3. **Put** toasted bagel slices side-by-side serving plate.

Make Peanut Butter Banana Bagel

1. **Spread** peanut butter over both halves of toasted bagel with plastic knife.

2. **Put** banana slices on top of peanut butter.

~ ENJOY!! ~

* When you finish cooking:
1. Put your ingredients and equipment away.
2. Wash and put your dishes away.
3. Wipe your cooking area clean.

Simple Sausage Patty

Makes 1 Sausage Patty

Make it a meal with scrambled eggs and bacon.

Gather Equipment

Put a paper towel on your cooking area to catch spills.

* Microwave

* 2 paper towels

* 1 serving plate

Gather Ingredients

* 1 breakfast sausage patty
  Buy a package of fully cooked sausage.

Cooking Directions

Prepare Sausage

1. **Put** 1 paper towel in microwave.

2. **Put** sausage patty on top of paper towel.

3. **Cover** sausage patty with 2nd paper towel.

Cook Sausage

1. **Microwave** sausage for 30 seconds.

2. **Remove** sausage from microwave.

3. **Put** sausage on serving plate.

~ ENJOY!! ~

FUN FACT More sausages are eaten on Saturday than any other day.

* When you finish cooking:
1. Put your ingredients and equipment away.
2. Wash and put your dishes away.
3. Wipe your cooking area clean.

Sticky Monkey Bread

Makes 10 Pieces

Best warm right out of the microwave. Pull apart and enjoy.

Gather Ingredients

* 4 tablespoons margarine

* ⅓ cup light brown sugar

* 1 teaspoon cinnamon

* 1 (16 ounce) can buttermilk biscuits

Gather Equipment

Put a paper towel on your cooking area to catch spills.

* Microwave

* 1 microwave-safe pie plate

* Measuring spoons

* ⅓ dry measuring cup

* 1 wooden spoon

* 1 cutting board

* 2 plastic knives
  Be safe: cut with a plastic knife.
  Use 1 knife to level ingredients.

* 2 pot holders

Cooking Directions

Make Sauce

1. **Measure** and **level** 4 tablespoons of margarine. **Put** into microwave-safe pie plate.

2. **Measure** and **level** ⅓ cup brown sugar in dry measuring cup. **Add** to margarine.

3. **Measure** and **level** 1 teaspoon cinnamon. **Add** to margarine.

4. **Microwave** 30 seconds. **Remove** from microwave with pot holders.

5. **Mix** with wooden spoon. **Set aside**.

Prepare Biscuits

1. **Open** buttermilk biscuit can. **Lay** each biscuit on cutting board.

2. **Cut** each biscuit into 4 pieces.
   Be safe: cut biscuits with a plastic knife.

3. **Put** 1 piece of biscuit into pie plate. **Turn** piece over in sauce.

4. **Continue** putting pieces, one at a time, into pie plate and turning over in sauce.

5. **Cover** bottom of pie plate with pieces. **Push** pieces together to fit.
   You may have a few pieces left over.

Cook Monkey Bread

1. **Microwave** 6 minutes at **70% Power**.

2. **Hit** the "power" button until it reads 7. Then **press** in 6 minutes for baking time.

3. **Remove** monkey bread from microwave with pot holders.

4. Best warm right out of the microwave.

~ ENJOY!! ~

*When you finish cooking:
1. Put your ingredients and equipment away.
2. Wash and put your dishes away.
3. Wipe your cooking area clean.

Favorite
Lunch & Dinner
Recipes

_____

_____

_____

_____

_____

_____

_____

_____

_____

_____

Balance your lunch and dinner

with fruits and vegetables

FUN FACT There are more than 600 different shapes of pasta!

FUN FACT October is National Pasta Month!

~ LUNCH & DINNER ~

A little more challenging

Bacon, Lettuce, Tomato Sandwich

Makes 1 Sandwich

This sandwich is a restaurant favorite and will be yours too.

Gather Ingredients

* 4 strips of bacon
  Buy a package of fully cooked bacon.

* 2 pieces of bread

* Mayonnaise for spreading

* 4 pieces lettuce

* 1 tomato

Gather Equipment

Put a paper towel on your cooking area to catch spills.

* Microwave and toaster

* 2 paper towels

* 1 cutting board

* 1 plastic knife
  Be safe: cut with a plastic knife.

* 1 serving plate

Cooking Directions

Cook Bacon

1. **Put** 2 paper towels on top of each other in the microwave.

2. **Lay** 4 bacon strips across paper towels.

3. **Microwave** bacon 1 minute. **Remove** bacon from microwave. **Set** aside.

Toast Bread

1. **Put** 2 pieces of bread in toaster. **Push** on.

2. **Put** toasted bread side-by-side on serving plate.

Make Sandwich

1. **Spread** 1 piece of toast with mayonnaise.

2. **Lay** 4 pieces of lettuce over mayonnaise.

3. **Cut** 4 thin slices of tomato on cutting board.
   Be safe: cut tomato with a plastic knife.

4. **Put** tomato slices side-by-side on lettuce.

5. **Put** 4 strips of bacon side-by-side on top of tomatoes.

6. **Put** 2nd piece of bread on top. **Cut** sandwich in half with plastic knife.

~ ENJOY!! ~

*When you finish cooking:
1. Put your ingredients and equipment away.
2. Wash and put your dishes away.
3. Wipe your cooking area clean.

Barbecue Chicken Sandwich

Makes 1 Sandwich

A barbecued sandwich without the work of a grill.

Gather Ingredients

* 3 defrosted chicken tenders

* ½ cup barbecue sauce

* 1 sliced sandwich roll

Gather Equipment

Put a paper towel on your cooking area to catch spills.

* Microwave

* 1 microwave-safe pie plate

* Plastic wrap

* 1 liquid measuring cup

* 1 kitchen tablespoon

* 1 kitchen fork

* 1 plastic knife
  Be safe: cut with a plastic knife.

* 1 serving plate

* 2 pot holders

Cooking Directions

Cook Chicken

1. **Put** 3 chicken tenders side-by-side in microwave-safe pie plate.

2. **Measure** ½ cup of barbecue sauce in liquid measuring cup.

3. **Pour** barbecue sauce over chicken.

4. **Smooth** sauce over chicken with back of kitchen tablespoon.
Cover "all" the chicken with barbecue sauce.

5. **Cover** pie plate with plastic wrap.

6. **Punch** 3 holes through plastic wrap with plastic knife.

7. **Microwave** chicken 5 minutes.

8. **Remove** chicken from microwave with pot holders.

9. **Wait** 2 minutes before removing plastic wrap.

10. **Remove** plastic wrap carefully. Steam will be hot.

Make Barbecue Sandwich

1. **Put** sandwich roll halves side-by-side on serving plate.

2. **Put** chicken on one half of sandwich roll.

3. **Spoon** a little extra barbeque sauce over chicken.

4. **Put** 2nd half of roll on top of chicken.

~ ENJOY!! ~

* When you finish cooking:
1. Put your ingredients and equipment away.
2. Wash and put your dishes away.
3. Wipe your cooking area clean.

Cheese Ravioli with Tomato Sauce

Makes 2 Servings

Add a green salad and garlic toast for the perfect pasta dinner.

Gather Ingredients

* 14 large cheese ravioli

* ¾ cup tomato sauce

* 2 tablespoons grated Parmesan cheese

Gather Equipment

Put a paper towel on your cooking area to catch spills.

* Microwave

* 1 large microwave-safe bowl
  (or pasta cooker*)

* 1 liquid measuring cup

* Measuring spoons

* 1 large slotted spoon
  A slotted spoon has holes in it.

* Wax paper

* 2 serving bowls

* 2 pot holders

*A Pasta Cooker can be purchased on-line. It is safer, faster and easier to use.

Cooking Directions

Cook Ravioli

1. **Measure** 6 cups water in liquid measuring cup.

2. **Pour** water into large microwave-safe bowl or pasta cooker.

3. **Add** 14 large cheese ravioli to water. **Microwave** 15 minutes. Do Not Cover.

Prepare Tomato Sauce *"while ravioli cooks"*

1. **Measure** ¾ cup tomato sauce in liquid measuring cup.

2. **Cover** sauce with a piece of wax paper. **Set aside.**

Mix Ravioli and Tomato Sauce

1. **Remove** cooked ravioli from microwave with pot holders. **Set aside.**

2. **Microwave** tomato sauce 1 minute. **Set aside.**

3. **Spoon** 7 ravioli into each serving bowl using large slotted spoon.

4. **Pour** 6 tablespoons tomato sauce over each bowl of ravioli.

5. **Sprinkle** each bowl with ½ tablespoon grated Parmesan cheese.

~ ENJOY!! ~

*When you finish cooking:
1. Put your ingredients and equipment away.
2. Wash and put your dishes away.
3. Wipe your cooking area clean.

Cheesy Quesadilla

Makes 1 Quesadilla

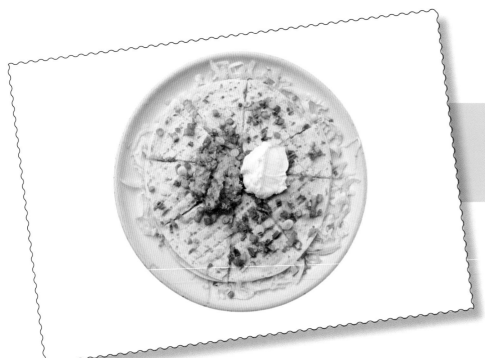

Fast! Easy! Delicious!

Gather Ingredients

* 2 medium flour tortillas

* ½ cup shredded Mexican cheese blend

* Your choice of toppings
    - 1 tablespoon sour cream
    - 1 tablespoon salsa
    - 1 tablespoon guacamole

Gather Equipment

Put a paper towel on your cooking area to catch spills.

* Microwave

* 1 microwave-safe plate

* 1 plastic knife
  Be safe: cut with a plastic knife.

* ½ dry measuring cup

* 2 pot holders

Cooking Directions

Make Quesadilla

1. **Place** 1 medium size tortilla on microwave-safe plate.

2. **Measure** ½ cup shredded Mexican cheese in dry measuring cup.

3. **Sprinkle** cheese over tortilla.

4. **Put** 2nd tortilla on top of cheese.

Cook Quesadilla

1. **Microwave** quesadilla for 30 seconds.

2. **Remove** quesadilla from microwave with pot holders.

3. **Cut** quesadilla in half. **Cut** each half in half. You should have 4 pieces.
   Be safe: cut quesadilla with a plastic knife.

Add Toppings

1. **Add** your choice of toppings
   - 1 tablespoon sour cream
   - 1 tablespoon salsa
   - 1 tablespoon guacamole

~ ENJOY!! ~

* When you finish cooking:
1. Put your ingredients and equipment away.
2. Wash and put your dishes away.
3. Wipe your cooking area clean.

Chick-a-Dee Quesadilla

Makes 1 Chicken Quesadilla

*Have left over chicken?
Add it to your quesadilla.*

Gather Equipment

Put a paper towel on your cooking area to catch spills.

* Microwave

* 1 microwave-safe plate

* ½ dry measuring cup

* 1 cutting board

* measuring spoons

* 1 plastic knife
  Be safe: cut with a plastic knife.

* 1 kitchen fork

* 2 pot holders

Gather Ingredients

* 2 medium flour tortillas

* ½ cup shredded Mexican cheese blend

* ½ cup cooked chicken
  About ½ a chicken breast.

* Your choice of toppings
  - 1 tablespoon sour cream
  - 1 tablespoon salsa
  - 1 tablespoon guacamole

Cooking Directions

Make Chicken Quesadilla

1. **Place** 1 medium tortilla on microwave-safe plate.

2. **Measure** ½ cup of shredded Mexican cheese in dry measuring cup.

3. **Sprinkle** cheese over tortilla.

4. **Cut** a ½ cup of chicken into small pieces on cutting board.
   Be safe: cut chicken with a plastic knife.

5. **Sprinkle** chicken pieces over cheese.

6. **Put** 2nd tortilla on top of chicken.

Cook Chicken Quesadilla

1. **Microwave** quesadilla for 30 seconds.

2. **Remove** quesadilla from microwave with pot holders.

3. **Cut** quesadilla in half. **Cut** each half in half. You should have 4 pieces.
   Be safe: cut quesadilla with a plastic knife.

Add Toppings

1. **Add** your choice of toppings
   - 1 tablespoon sour cream
   - 1 tablespoon salsa
   - 1 tablespoon guacamole

~ ENJOY!! ~

*When you finish cooking:
1. Put your ingredients and equipment away.
2. Wash and put your dishes away.
3. Wipe your cooking area clean.

Chicken Salad Sandwich

Makes 1 Sandwich

An old time favorite.

Gather Ingredients

* 1 (5 ounce) can white chicken in water
* 1 tablespoon relish
* 2 tablespoons mayonnaise
* 2 pieces of bread

Gather Equipment

Put a paper towel on your cooking area to catch spills.

* 1 colander
* 1 small mixing bowl
* 1 can opener
* 1 kitchen fork
* 1 kitchen teaspoon
* 1 plastic knife
  Be safe: cut with a plastic knife.
* Measuring spoons
* 1 serving plate
* Plastic wrap

Cooking Directions

Make Chicken Salad

1. **Put** colander in sink. **Open** (5 ounce) can of chicken.

2. **Empty** chicken into colander. **Let** water drain out.

3. **Pour** chicken into small mixing bowl.

4. **Break** up chicken chunks with kitchen fork.

5. **Measure** 1 tablespoon of relish. Add to chicken.

6. **Measure** 2 tablespoons of mayonnaise. Add to chicken.

7. **Mix** with kitchen fork.

Make Chicken Salad Sandwich

1. **Put** 2 pieces bread on plate side-by-side.

2. **Scoop** and **spread** enough chicken salad to cover 1 piece of bread.

3. **Put** 2nd piece of bread over chicken salad. **Cut** sandwich in half.
   Be safe: cut sandwich with a plastic knife.

Leftovers

1. **Cover** leftover chicken salad with plastic wrap and put in refrigerator.

~ ENJOY!! ~

*When you finish cooking:
1. Put your ingredients and equipment away.
2. Wash and put your dishes away.
3. Wipe your cooking area clean.

Chicken Tenders

Makes 2 Servings

Add a veggie and a potato for a well balanced meal.

Gather Equipment

Put a paper towel on your cooking area to catch spills.

* Microwave

* 1 8x8 square microwave-safe dish

* Plastic wrap

* 1 liquid measuring cup

* 1 plastic knife

* 2 pot holders

Gather Ingredients

* 6 defrosted chicken tenders

* ¾ cup chicken broth
  Chicken broth from a carton is easier to pour.

Cooking Directions

Prepare Chicken

1. **Put** 6 chicken tenders side-by-side in 8x8 microwave-safe dish.

2. **Measure** ¾ cup of chicken broth in liquid measuring cup.

3. **Pour** chicken broth over chicken.

4. **Cover** dish with plastic wrap.

5. **Punch** 3 holes through plastic wrap with plastic knife.

Cook Chicken

1. **Microwave** chicken 5 minutes.

2. **Remove** chicken from microwave with pot holders.

3. **Wait** 2 minutes before removing plastic wrap.

4. **Remove** plastic wrap carefully. Steam will be hot.

~ ENJOY!! ~

Cook only 2 chicken tenders to add some chicken to a favorite recipe . . .

* Chick-a-Dee Quesadilla, page 44
* Pasta and Peas with Alfredo Sauce, page 58
* Tortellini with Pesto Sauce, page 64
* Chicken Orzo Soup, page 68
* Potato and Corn Parmesan Soup, page 80
* Tortellini Pesto Soup, page 86

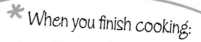

* When you finish cooking:
1. Put your ingredients and equipment away.
2. Wash and put your dishes away.
3. Wipe your cooking area clean.

Chili Cheese Dog

Makes 1 Chili Cheese Dog

Make and enjoy a chili dog right at home!

Gather Ingredients

* 1 hot dog bun

* 1 hot dog

* 3 tablespoons canned chili

* 1 tablespoon shredded Cheddar cheese

Gather Equipment

Put a paper towel on your cooking area to catch spills.

* Microwave

* 1 paper towel

* 1 kitchen fork

* Measuring spoons

* 1 can opener

* 1 microwave-safe serving plate

Cooking Directions

Cook Hot Dog

1. **Remove** 1 hot dog from package.

2. **Punch** hot dog 2 times with kitchen fork.

3. **Wrap** hot dog in 1 paper towel. **Microwave** 30 seconds.

4. **Remove** hot dog from microwave.

5. **Put** hot dog in bun on microwave-safe serving plate.

Make Chili Cheese Dog

1. **Open** can of chili.

2. **Spoon** and **spread** 3 tablespoons of chili over hot dog.

3. **Sprinkle** 1 tablespoon shredded cheddar cheese over chili.

4. **Microwave** chili cheese dog for 20 seconds.

5. **Remove** chili dog from microwave with pot holders.

~ ENJOY!! ~

* When you finish cooking:
1. Put your ingredients and equipment away.
2. Wash and put your dishes away.
3. Wipe your cooking area clean.

Garlic Cheddar Cheese Toast

Makes 6 Pieces

Wonderful with pasta.

Gather Ingredients

* ¼ cup shredded Cheddar cheese

* 2 tablespoons margarine

* ¼ teaspoon minced garlic
  Garlic from a jar is easier to use.

* 2 tablespoons mayonnaise

* ⅛ teaspoon salt

* 2 dashes white pepper

* 6 pieces sliced Italian bread

Gather Equipment

Put a paper towel on your cooking area to catch spills.

* Microwave and toaster

* 1 small mixing bowl

* 1 kitchen teaspoon

* 1 kitchen knife

* 1 plastic knife
  Use knife to level ingredients.

* Measuring spoons

* ¼ dry measuring cup

* 1 large microwave-safe serving plate

Cooking Directions

Make Garlic Spread

1. **Measure** ¼ cup shredded Cheddar cheese in dry measuring cup.

2. **Pour** cheese into small mixing bowl.

3. **Measure** and **level** 2 tablespoons margarine. **Add** to cheese.

4. **Measure** and **level** ¼ teaspoon minced garlic from a jar. **Add** to cheese.

5. **Measure** and **level** 2 tablespoons mayonnaise. **Add** to cheese.

6. **Measure** and **level** ⅛ teaspoon salt. **Add** to cheese.

7. **Add** 2 dashes white pepper to cheese. **Mix** with kitchen teaspoon. **Set** aside.

Toast Bread and Add Garlic Spread

1. **Put** 2 pieces of sliced Italian bread in toaster. **Push** on.

2. **Put** toasted bread on large microwave-safe serving plate.

3. **Spread** garlic Cheddar cheese spread on toast using kitchen knife.

4. **Continue** toasting and spreading until the 6 pieces of bread are done.

Cook Garlic Cheddar Cheese Toast

1. **Microwave** plate of toast for 15 seconds to melt cheese.

2. **Remove** plate from microwave.

~ ENJOY!! ~

* When you finish cooking:
1. Put your ingredients and equipment away.
2. Wash and put your dishes away.
3. Wipe your cooking area clean.

Ham and Cheese Croissant

Makes 1 Sandwich

A croissant turns a plain ham and cheese sandwich into a real treat.

Gather Ingredients

* 1 croissant

* Mayonnaise for spreading

* 4 pieces lettuce

* 3 slices deli ham

* 2 slices Provolone cheese

* 1 tomato

Gather Equipment

Put a paper towel on your cooking area to catch spills.

* 1 plastic knife
  Be safe: cut with a plastic knife

* 1 cutting board

* 1 serving plate

Cooking Directions

Make Sandwich

1. **Cut** croissant in half on cutting board. **Lay** croissant halves side-by-side.
   Be safe: cut croissant with a plastic knife.

2. **Spread** mayonnaise over 1 half of croissant with plastic knife.

3. **Lay** 4 pieces of lettuce over mayonnaise.

4. **Lay** 3 slices of deli ham over lettuce.

5. **Put** 2 slices Provolone cheese on top of ham.

6. **Cut** 3 thin slices of tomato on cutting board.
   Be safe: cut tomato with a plastic knife.

7. **Put** tomato slices side-by-side on top of cheese.

8. **Put** 2nd half of croissant on top. **Put** sandwich on serving plate.

~ ENJOY!! ~

* When you finish cooking:
1. Put your ingredients and equipment away.
2. Wash and put your dishes away.
3. Wipe your cooking area clean.

Hot Diggity Dog

Makes 1 Hot Dog

Lunch is ready in less than a minute.

Gather Ingredients

* 1 hot dog bun

* 1 hot dog

* Your choice of toppings
    - ½ tablespoon mustard
    - ½ tablespoon relish
    - ½ tablespoon ketchup

Gather Equipment

Put a paper towel on your cooking area to catch spills.

* Microwave

* 1 kitchen fork

* Measuring spoons

* 1 paper towel

* 1 serving plate

Cooking Directions

Cook Hot Dog

1. **Remove** 1 hot dog from package.

2. **Punch** hot dog 2 times with kitchen fork.

3. **Wrap** hot dog in 1 paper towel. **Microwave** 30 seconds.

4. **Remove** hot dog from microwave.

5. **Put** hot dog in bun on serving plate.

Add Toppings

1. **Add** your choice of toppings
   - ½ tablespoon mustard
   - ½ tablespoon relish
   - ½ tablespoon ketchup

~ ENJOY!! ~

FUN FACT July is National Hot Dog Month!

* When you finish cooking:
1. Put your ingredients and equipment away.
2. Wash and put your dishes away.
3. Wipe your cooking area clean.

Pasta and Peas with Alfredo Sauce

Makes 2 Servings

Pasta, pasta everyone screams for pasta!

Gather Equipment

Put a paper towel on your cooking area to catch spills.

* Microwave
* 1 large microwave-safe bowl (or pasta cooker*)
* 1 small microwave-safe bowl
* 1 liquid measuring cup
* Dry measuring cups
* Measuring spoons
* 1 wooden spoon
* 1 large serving spoon
* 1 colander
* Wax paper
* 1 kitchen teaspoon
* 2 pot holders

*A pasta cooker can be purchased on-line. It is safer, faster and easier to use.

Gather Ingredients

* 3 cups rotini or bow pasta
* ½ cup Alfredo sauce
* 1 cup frozen peas

Cooking Directions

Cook Pasta

1. **Measure** 6 cups water in liquid measuring cup.

2. **Pour** water into large microwave-safe bowl or pasta cooker.

3. **Measure** 3 cups pasta in dry measuring cup. **Add** to water.

4. **Mix** with wooden spoon. **Microwave** 15 minutes. Do Not Cover

Prepare Sauce and Peas *"while pasta cooks"*

1. **Measure** ½ cup Alfredo sauce in dry measuring cup.

2. **Pour** Alfredo sauce into small microwave-safe bowl.

3. **Cover** sauce with piece of wax paper. **Set aside.**

4. **Measure** 1 cup frozen peas in liquid measuring cup. **Add** ½ tablespoon water to peas.

5. **Cover** peas with a piece of wax paper. **Set aside.**

Mix Pasta, Sauce and Peas

1. **Remove** cooked pasta from microwave with pot holders. **Set aside.**

2. **Microwave** Alfredo sauce 30 seconds. **Set aside.**

3. **Microwave** peas 1 minute and 30 seconds. **Set aside.**

4. **Put** colander in sink. **Pour** pasta into colander. **Let** water drain.

5. **Pour** pasta back into microwave-safe bowl or pasta cooker.

6. **Add** Alfredo sauce and peas to pasta. **Mix** with wooden spoon.

~ ENJOY!! ~

*When you finish cooking:
1. Put your ingredients and equipment away.
2. Wash and put your dishes away.
3. Wipe your cooking area clean.

Salsa Chicken

Makes 2 Servings

Not too spicy chicken Mexican style.

Gather Ingredients

* ⅓ cup salsa

* 2 tablespoons medium spice taco sauce

* ⅛ teaspoon salt

* 6 defrosted chicken tenders

* ⅓ cup shredded Mexican cheese blend

Gather Equipment

Put a paper towel on your cooking area to catch spills.

* Microwave

* 1 8x8 square microwave-safe dish

* Measuring spoons

* ⅓ dry measuring cup

* 1 small mixing bowl

* 1 kitchen tablespoon

* 1 plastic knife
  Use knife to level ingredients.

* Plastic wrap

* 2 pot holders

Cooking Directions

Make Sauce

1. **Measure** ⅓ cup salsa in dry measuring cup. **Add** to small mixing bowl.

2. **Measure** 2 tablespoons taco sauce. **Add** to salsa.

3. **Measure** and **level** ⅛ teaspoon salt. **Add** to salsa.

4. **Mix** sauce with kitchen tablespoon. **Set aside.**

Cook Salsa Chicken

1. **Place** 6 chicken tenders side-by-side in 8x8 microwave-safe dish.

2. **Pour** salsa sauce over chicken.

3. **Smooth** sauce over chicken with back of kitchen tablespoon.
   Cover "all" the chicken with sauce.

4. **Measure** ⅓ cup shredded Mexican cheese in dry measuring cup.

5. **Sprinkle** cheese over chicken.

6. **Cover** dish with plastic wrap. **Microwave** 5 minutes.

7. **Remove** chicken from microwave with pot holders.

8. **Wait** 2 minutes before removing plastic wrap.

9. **Remove** plastic wrap carefully. Steam will be hot.

~ ENJOY!! ~

* When you finish cooking:
1. Put your ingredients and equipment away.
2. Wash and put your dishes away.
3. Wipe your cooking area clean.

Sweet and Sour Chicken

Makes 2 Servings

You make the chicken + a friend makes the salad = dinner is ready.

Gather Equipment

Put a paper towel on your cooking area to catch spills.

* Microwave

* 1 8x8 microwave-safe dish

* 1 kitchen tablespoon

* 1 medium mixing bowl

* 1 liquid measuring cup

* Plastic wrap

* 2 pot holders

Gather Ingredients

* 1 package dry onion soup mix

* 1 (12 ounce) jar apricot preserves

* 1 cup Thousand Island salad dressing

* 6 defrosted chicken tenders

Cooking Directions

Make Sauce

1. **Empty** 1 package onion soup mix into medium mixing bowl.

2. **Add** (12-ounce) jar apricot preserves to onion soup mix.

3. **Measure** 1 cup Thousand Island salad dressing in liquid measuring cup.

4. **Add** salad dressing to onion soup mix.

5. **Mix** with kitchen tablespoon. **Set aside.**

Cook Sweet & Sour Chicken

1. **Lay** chicken tenders side-by-side in 8x8 microwave-safe dish.

2. **Pour** sauce over chicken.

3. **Smooth** sauce over chicken with back of kitchen tablespoon.
   Cover "all" the chicken with sauce.

4. **Cover** dish with plastic wrap. **Microwave** 10 minutes.

5. **Remove** chicken from microwave with pot holders.

6. **Wait** 2 minutes before removing plastic wrap.

7. **Remove** plastic wrap carefully. Steam will be hot.

~ ENJOY!! ~

* When you finish cooking:
1. Put your ingredients and equipment away.
2. Wash and put your dishes away.
3. Wipe your cooking area clean.

Tortellini with Pesto Sauce

Makes 2 Servings

Light, little cheese rolls.

Gather Ingredients

* 1 (9 ounce) package refrigerated cheese tortellini

* ¼ cup pesto sauce

* 1 tablespoon grated Parmesan cheese

Gather Equipment

Put a paper towel on your cooking area to catch spills

* Microwave

* 1 large microwave-safe bowl
  (or pasta cooker*)

* 1 liquid measuring cup

* ¼ dry measuring cup

* 1 wooden spoon

* 1 large serving spoon

* Wax paper

* 1 colander

* 2 serving bowls

* 2 pot holders

*A pasta cooker can be purchased on-line. It is safer, easier and faster to use.

Cooking Directions

Cook Tortellini

1. **Measure** 6 cups water in liquid measuring cup.

2. **Pour** water into microwave-safe bowl or pasta cooker.

3. **Add** (9 ounce) package of tortellini to water. **Mix** with wooden spoon.

4. **Microwave** 15 minutes. Do Not Cover.

Prepare Pesto Sauce *"while tortellini cooks"*

1. **Measure** ¼ cup pesto sauce in dry measuring cup. **Set aside.**
Pesto Sauce does not have to be cooked.

Mix Tortellini and Pesto Sauce

1. **Put** colander in sink.

2. **Remove** cooked tortellini from microwave with pot holders.

3. **Pour** tortellini into colander. **Let** water drain.

4. **Pour** tortellini back into microwave-safe bowl or pasta cooker.

5. **Add** pesto sauce to tortellini. **Mix** with wooden spoon.

6. **Spoon** tortellini into 2 serving bowls with large serving spoon.

7. **Sprinkle** each bowl with ½ tablespoon of grated Parmesan cheese.

~ ENJOY!! ~

*When you finish cooking:
1. Put your ingredients and equipment away.
2. Wash and put your dishes away.
3. Wipe your cooking area clean.

Favorite Soup & Salad Recipes

dessert entree

Healthy Comfort Food

Warm Soup, Crispy Salad, and a Tasty Roll

FUN FACT Honey is the only food on the planet that will not spoil or rot!

FUN FACT In 1887 the US Supreme Court ruled that tomatoes were vegetables.

~ SOUPS & SALADS ~

*A little more challenging

Chicken Orzo Soup

Makes 4 Servings

Chicken and Italian rice soup. Mmm, Mmm good!

Gather Ingredients

* 1 (32 ounce) container chicken broth

* 1 (5 ounce) container chopped carrots, celery & onion

* ¼ cup orzo (Italian Rice)

* ½ cup frozen peas

* 1 cup cooked chicken
About 1 chicken breast

Gather Equipment

Put a paper towel on your cooking area to catch spills.

* Microwave

* 1 large microwave-safe bowl (or pasta cooker*)

* 1 wooden spoon

* Dry measuring cups

* 1 plastic knife Be safe: cut with a plastic knife.

* 1 cutting board

* 4 soup bowls

* 1 soup ladle

* 2 pot holders

*A pasta cooker can be purchased on-line. It is safer, easier and faster to use.

Cooking Directions

Begin Making Soup

1. **Open** (32 ounce) container chicken broth.

2. **Pour** broth into large microwave-safe bowl or pasta cooker.

3. **Add** (5 ounce) container of chopped carrots, celery, and onion to chicken broth.

4. **Stir** soup with wooden spoon.

Cook Soup

1. **Microwave** soup 15 minutes. Do Not Cover

Prepare Orzo, Peas and Chicken *"while broth and vegetables are cooking"*

1. **Measure** ¼ cup orzo in dry measuring cup. **Set aside.**

2. **Measure** ½ cup frozen peas in dry measuring cup. **Set aside.**

3. **Cut** 1 cup cooked chicken breast into small pieces on cutting board. **Set aside**
   Be safe: cut chicken with a plastic knife.

Add Orzo, Peas, and Chicken

1. **Remove** soup from microwave with pot holders. **Stir** soup with wooden spoon.

2. **Add** orzo, peas, and chicken pieces.

3. **Stir** soup with wooden spoon.

Cook Soup

1. **Microwave** soup 15 minutes. **Remove** soup from microwave with pot holders.

2. **Stir** soup with wooden spoon.

Serve Soup

1. **Ladle** soup into 4 soup bowls.

~ ENJOY!! ~

*When you finish cooking:
1. Put your ingredients and equipment away.
2. Wash and put your dishes away.
3. Wipe your cooking area clean.

Cranberry Walnut Salad

Makes 4 Salads

Easy and Delicious!

Gather Equipment

Put a paper towel on your cooking area to catch spills.

* 4 small salad bowls

* Measuring spoons

* 1 small bowl
  Catch spills: measure over bowl.

Gather Ingredients

* 1 bag of washed spring salad mix

* 4 tablespoons dried cranberries

* 4 tablespoons candied walnuts

* 4 tablespoons crumbled feta cheese

* 4 tablespoons cranberry walnut salad dressing

Cooking Directions

Prepare Salad Mix

1. **Open** package of washed spring salad mix.

2. **Divide** leaves into 4 small salad bowls.

Add Salad Toppings

1. **Sprinkle** 1 tablespoon dried cranberries on each salad.

2. **Sprinkle** 1 tablespoon candied walnuts on each salad.

3. **Sprinkle** 1 tablespoon crumbled feta cheese on each salad.

4. **Sprinkle** 1 tablespoon cranberry walnut salad dressing on each salad.
   Catch spills: measure dressing over a small bowl, then sprinkle on salad.

~ ENJOY!! ~

FUN FACT Cranberries are also know as "bounceberries"—they bounce when ripe.

✻ When you finish cooking:
1. Put your ingredients and equipment away.
2. Wash and put your dishes away.
3. Wipe your cooking area clean.

Creamy Tomato and Rice Basil Soup

Makes 4 Servings

Add a green salad,
a roll and make this
soup a complete meal.

Gather Equipment

Put a paper towel on your cooking area to catch spills.

* Microwave

* 1 large microwave-safe bowl
  (or Pasta Cooker*)

* 1 wooden spoon

* 1 can opener

* Measuring spoons

* 1 cup dry measuring cup

* 1 soup ladle

* 2 pot holders

* 4 soup bowls

*A Pasta Cooker can be purchased on-line. It is safer, easier and faster to use.

Gather Ingredients

* 1 (28 ounce) can crushed tomatoes

* 1 (32 ounce) container vegetable broth

* 1 cup instant rice

* 1 pint heavy cream

* 1 teaspoon dried basil

* Salt and pepper shakers

* 4 tablespoons shredded Parmesan cheese

Cooking Directions

Begin Making Soup

1. **Open** (28 ounce) can crushed tomatoes.

2. **Pour** into large microwave-safe bowl or pasta cooker.

3. **Open** (32 ounce) container vegetable broth. **Add** to crushed tomatoes.

4. **Measure** 1 cup instant rice in dry measuring cup. **Add** to crushed tomatoes.

5. **Stir** soup with wooden spoon.

Cook Soup

1. **Microwave** soup 5 minutes. **Remove** soup from microwave with pot holders.

Add Cream and Seasonings

1. **Open** 1 pint heavy cream. **Add** to soup.

2. **Measure** 1 teaspoon basil. **Add** to soup.

3. **Add** 2 dashes of salt and pepper to soup.

4. **Stir** soup with wooden spoon.

Cook Soup

1. **Microwave** soup 7 minutes. **Remove** soup from microwave with pot holders.

Serve Soup

1. **Ladle** soup into 4 soup bowls.

2. **Sprinkle** each bowl with 1 tablespoon of shredded Parmesan cheese.

~ ENJOY!! ~

*When you finish cooking:
1. Put your ingredients and equipment away.
2. Wash and put your dishes away.
3. Wipe your cooking area clean.

Crunchy Coleslaw

Makes 4 Servings

Coleslaw is great with a hot dog or a sandwich.

Gather Ingredients

* ½ cup mayonnaise

* 1 tablespoon cider vinegar

* 2 teaspoons sugar

* ½ teaspoon salt

* ½ teaspoon celery seed

* 1 (16 ounce) package of 3-color Coleslaw

Gather Equipment

Put a paper towel on your cooking area to catch spills.

* 1 large salad bowl

* 1 small mixing bowl

* 1 small bowl
  Catch spills: measure over bowl.

* 1 plastic knife
  Use knife to level ingredients.

* 1 wooden spoon

* Measuring spoons

* ½ dry measuring cup

* Plastic wrap

Cooking Directions

Make Salad Dressing

1. **Measure** and **level** ½ cup mayonnaise in dry measuring cup.

2. **Pour** mayonnaise into small mixing bowl.

3. **Measure** 1 tablespoon cider vinegar. **Add** to mayonnaise.
   Catch spills: measure vinegar over small bowl, then add to mayonnaise.

4. **Measure** and **level** 2 teaspoons sugar. **Add** to mayonnaise.

5. **Measure** and **level** ½ teaspoon salt. **Add** to mayonnaise.

6. **Measure** and **level** ½ teaspoon celery seed. **Add** to mayonnaise.

7. **Mix** with wooden spoon. **Set aside.**

Make Salad

1. **Empty** (16 ounce) 3-color Coleslaw mix into large salad bowl.

2. **Pour** dressing over Coleslaw. **Mix** with wooden spoon.

3. **Cover** with plastic wrap.

4. **Refrigerate** until ready to serve.

~ ENJOY!! ~

* When you finish cooking:
1. Put your ingredients and equipment away.
2. Wash and put your dishes away.
3. Wipe your cooking area clean.

Delicious Green Salad

Makes 4 Salads

A delicious green salad is healthy with any meal.

Gather Ingredients

* 1 bag of washed spring salad mix

* 16 cherry tomatoes

* 4 tablespoons shredded Parmesan cheese

* 4 tablespoons of your favorite salad dressing

Gather Equipment

Put a paper towel on your cooking area to catch spills.

* 4 small salad bowls

* 1 plastic knife
  Be safe: cut with a plastic knife.

* 1 cutting board

* Measuring spoons

* 1 colander

Cooking Directions

Prepare Salad Mix

1. **Open** package of washed spring salad mix.

2. **Divide** leaves into 4 small salad bowls.

Add Tomatoes

1. **Put** colander in sink. **Put** 16 cherry tomatoes in colander. **Rinse** with cold water.

2. **Cut** cherry tomatoes in half on cutting board.
   Be safe: cut tomatoes with a plastic knife.

3. **Put** 8 tomato pieces on top of each salad.

Add Salad Toppings

1. **Sprinkle** 1 tablespoon shredded Parmesan cheese on each salad.

2. **Sprinkle** 1 tablespoon of your favorite salad dressing on each salad.

~ ENJOY!! ~

* When you finish cooking:
1. Put your ingredients and equipment away.
2. Wash and put your dishes away.
3. Wipe your cooking area clean.

Healthy Fruit Salad

Makes 4 Servings

A little honey adds a delightful taste to this summer salad.

Gather Ingredients

* 1 (16 ounce) basket strawberries
* 1 (6 ounce) basket blueberries
* 1 small bunch green grapes
* 1 small container cantaloupe chunks
* ½ tablespoon honey
* 1 small orange

Gather Equipment

Put a paper towel on your cooking area to catch spills.

* 1 medium mixing bowl
* 1 small bowl Catch spills: measure over bowl.
* 1 plastic knife Be safe: cut with a plastic knife.
* 1 wooden spoon
* Measuring spoons
* 1 cutting board
* 1 colander
* 4 paper towels
* 1 cookie sheet

Cooking Directions

Wash Fruit

1. **Cover** cookie sheet with 4 paper towels. **Set aside.**

2. **Put** colander in sink. **Pour** strawberries and blueberries into colander.

3. **Pull** grapes off of stems. **Add** grapes to colander.

4. **Rinse** fruit with cold water. **Empty** fruit onto cookie sheet.

5. **Spread** fruit over cookie sheet.

Prepare Fruit

1. **Check** blueberries for stems. **Remove** stems.

2. **Add** blueberries and grapes to medium mixing bowl.

3. **Cut** stems off strawberries on cutting board.
   Be safe: cut strawberry stems off with a plastic knife.

4. **Cut** strawberries into 4 pieces. **Add** to fruit in bowl.
   Be safe: cut strawberries with a plastic knife.

5. **Cut** cantaloupe chunks into 4 pieces on cutting board. **Add** to fruit in bowl.
   Be safe: cut cantaloupe with a plastic knife.

Add Salad Dressing

1. **Measure** ½ tablespoon honey. **Add** to fruit in bowl.
   Catch spills: Measure honey over a small bowl, then add to bowl.

2. **Cut** orange in half with plastic knife on cutting board.

3. **Squeeze** juice out of orange with your hand over fruit in bowl.

4. **Mix** with wooden spoon.

~ ENJOY!! ~

* When you finish cooking:
1. Put your ingredients and equipment away.
2. Wash and put your dishes away.
3. Wipe your cooking area clean.

Potato and Corn Parmesan Soup

Makes 4 Servings

Comfort food: warm soup, crispy salad, tasty roll.

Gather Equipment

Put a paper towel on your cooking area to catch spills.

* Microwave

* 1 large microwave-safe bowl
  (or pasta cooker*)

* 1 cup dry measuring cup

* 1 liquid measuring cup

* 1 wooden spoon

* 1 colander

* 1 can opener

* 1 soup ladle

* 4 soup bowls

* 2 pot holders

*A Pasta Cooker can be purchased on-line. It is safer, easier and faster to use.

Gather Ingredients

* 2 cups instant potato flakes

* 1 (32 ounce) container chicken broth

* ½ cup half-and-half cream

* 1 (11 ounce) can corn

* 1 cup shredded Parmesan cheese

* Pepper shaker

Cooking Directions

Begin Making Soup

1. **Measure** 2 cups instant potato flakes in dry measuring cup.

2. **Pour** potato flakes into large microwave-safe bowl or pasta cooker.

3. **Open** (32 ounce) container chicken broth. **Add** to potato flakes.

4. **Measure** ½ cup half-and-half in liquid measuring cup. **Add** to potato flakes.

5. **Set aside.**

Add Corn

1. **Put** colander in sink.

2. **Open** (11 ounce) can of corn. **Pour** corn into colander. **Let** water drain.

3. **Add** corn to soup. **Stir** soup with wooden spoon.

Cook Soup

1. **Microwave** soup 3 minutes. **Remove** soup from microwave with pot holders.

Add Cheese and Seasoning

1. **Add** 1 cup of shredded Parmesan cheese to soup.

2. **Add** 2 dashes pepper to soup.

3. **Stir** soup with wooden spoon.

Cook Soup

1. **Microwave** soup 1 minute. **Remove** soup from microwave with pot holders.

2. **Stir** soup with wooden spoon.

Serve Soup

1. **Ladle** soup into 4 soup bowls.

~ ENJOY!! ~

* When you finish cooking:
1. Put your ingredients and equipment away.
2. Wash and put your dishes away.
3. Wipe your cooking area clean.

Sweet Cheery Tomato Salad

Makes 4 Salads

The herbs make an awesome salad dressing.

Gather Equipment

Put a paper towel on your cooking area to catch spills.

* 1 medium mixing bowl

* 1 cutting board

* 2 plastic knives
  Be safe: cut with a plastic knife.
  Use to level ingredients.

* Measuring spoons

* 1 small bowl Catch spills: measure over bowl.

* 1 colander

* 1 wooden spoon

* 4 salad bowls

* 1 large serving spoon

Gather Ingredients

* 1 tablespoon olive oil

* ⅛ teaspoon dry basil

* ⅛ teaspoon dry chives

* ⅛ teaspoon dry tarragon

* Salt and pepper shakers

* 1 bag of washed spring salad mix

* 1 basket cherry tomatoes

Cooking Directions

Make Salad Dressing

1. **Measure** 1 tablespoon olive oil. **Add** to medium mixing bowl.
Catch spills: measure olive oil over a small bowl, then add to mixing bowl.

2. **Measure** and **level** ⅛ teaspoon basil. **Add** to olive oil.

3. **Measure** and **level** ⅛ teaspoon chives. **Add** to olive oil.

4. **Measure** and **level** ⅛ teaspoon tarragon. **Add** to olive oil.

5. **Add** 3 dashes of salt and pepper to olive oil.

6. **Mix** with wooden spoon. **Set aside.**

Prepare Tomatoes

1. **Put** colander in sink.

2. **Put** 1 basket cherry tomatoes into colander. **Rinse** with cold water.

3. **Cut** tomatoes in half on cutting board. **Add** tomatoes to salad dressing.
Be safe: cut tomatoes with a plastic knife.

4. **Mix** gently with wooden spoon. **Set aside.**

Make Salad

1. **Open** package of washed spring salad mix.

2. **Divide** leaves into 4 small salad bowls.

3. **Spoon** tomatoes on each salad with large serving spoon.

~ ENJOY!! ~

*When you finish cooking:
1. Put your ingredients and equipment away.
2. Wash and put your dishes away.
3. Wipe your cooking area clean.

Tomato and Feta Cheese Salad

Makes 4 Servings

This tomato salad looks beautiful on the table.

Gather Ingredients

* 6 Italian plum tomatoes

* ¼ cup olive oil

* ½ tablespoon dried basil

* 1 (4 ounce) container crumbled Feta cheese

Gather Equipment

Put a paper towel on your cooking area to catch spills.

* 1 serving platter

* 1 cutting board

* 1 plastic knife
  Be safe: cut with a plastic knife.

* 1 liquid measuring cup

* Measuring spoons

Cooking Directions

Prepare Tomatoes

1. **Rinse** tomatoes with cold water in sink.

2. **Cut** tomatoes into thick slices on cutting board. **Throw** ends away.
   Be safe: cut tomatoes with a plastic knife.

3. **Put** sliced tomatoes in rows on serving platter.

Add Salad Toppings

1. **Measure** ¼ cup olive oil in liquid measuring cup.

2. **Drizzle** over *"all"* the tomatoes.

3. **Measure** ½ tablespoon basil. **Sprinkle** over *"all"* the tomatoes.

4. **Sprinkle** 4-ounce container crumbled feta cheese over *"all"* the tomatoes.

~ ENJOY!! ~

To make it easier to drizzle olive oil . . .

Use a funnel to pour the olive oil into an empty plastic travel container that has a small hole on top. Then drizzle the olive oil over the tomatoes.

*When you finish cooking:
1. Put your ingredients and equipment away.
2. Wash and put your dishes away.
3. Wipe your cooking area clean.

Tortellini Pesto Soup

Makes 2 Servings

You'll want to have this fabulous soup over and over.

Gather Equipment

Put a paper towel on your cooking area to catch spills.

* Microwave
* 1 large microwave-safe bowl (or pasta cooker*)
* 1 can opener
* Dry measuring cups
* Measuring spoons
* 1 wooden spoon
* 1 colander
* 1 kitchen teaspoon
* 1 Soup ladle
* 2 soup bowls
* 2 pot holders

*A Pasta Cooker can be purchased on-line. It is safer, easier and faster to use.

Gather Ingredients

* 1 (32 ounce) container chicken broth
* 1 (14.5 ounce) can petite cut tomatoes
* 1 (9 ounce) packaged refrigerated cheese tortellini
* ⅓ cup pesto
* 2 tablespoons shredded Parmesan cheese

Cooking Directions

Begin Making Soup

1. **Open** (32 ounce) container chicken broth.

2. **Pour** into large microwave-safe bowl or pasta cooker. **Set aside.**

Add Tomatoes and Tortellini

1. **Put** colander into sink. **Open** (14.5 ounce) can petite cut tomatoes.

2. **Pour** tomatoes into colander. **Let** juice drain.

3. **Measure** ½ cup of drained tomatoes in dry measuring cup.

4. **Add** tomatoes to chicken broth.

5. **Open** (9 ounce) package tortellini. **Add** to chicken broth.

6. **Stir** soup with wooden spoon.

Cook Soup

1. **Microwave** soup 15 minutes. Remove soup from microwave with pot holders.

Add Pesto

1. **Measure** ⅓ cup pesto in dry measuring cup. **Add** to soup.

2. **Stir** soup with wooden spoon.

Serve Soup

1. **Ladle** soup into 2 soup bowls.

2. **Sprinkle** each bowl with 1 tablespoon shredded Parmesan cheese.

 ~ ENJOY!! ~

 *When you finish cooking:
1. Put your ingredients and equipment away.
2. Wash and put your dishes away.
3. Wipe your cooking area clean.

Favorite
Dessert
Recipes

_____

_____

_____

_____

_____

_____

_____

_____

_____

_____

"There is nothing better than a friend, unless it is a
friend with chocolate." — Charles Dickens

FUN FACT Hershey is the oldest and largest chocolate factory in the US.

FUN FACT Melted chocolate all over your hands means you're eating it too slowly!

~ DESSERT ~

A little more challenging

Chocolate Marshmallow Pudding

Makes 4 Servings

A fun and easy dessert.

Gather Ingredients

* 1 (3.4 ounce) instant chocolate pudding mix

* 2 cups milk

* 1½ cups mini marshmallows

Gather Equipment

Put a paper towel on your cooking area to catch spills.

* 1 large mixing bowl

* 1 liquid measuring cup

* Dry measuring cups

* 1 whisk

* 1 wooden spoon

* Timer

Cooking Directions

Make Pudding

1. **Open** (3.4 ounce) package of instant chocolate pudding mix.

2. **Pour** pudding mix into large mixing bowl.

3. **Measure** 2 cups milk in liquid measuring cup. **Add** to pudding mix.

4. **Mix** with whisk for 2 minutes. Set timer.

Add Marshmallows

1. **Measure** 1½ cups mini marshmallows in dry measuring cups.

2. **Add** marshmallows to pudding.

3. **Mix** with wooden spoon.

4. **Wait** 5 minutes before serving. Set timer.

~ ENJOY!! ~

*When you finish cooking:
1. Put your ingredients and equipment away.
2. Wash and put your dishes away.
3. Wipe your cooking area clean.

Chocolate Mug Cake

Makes 1 Mug Cake

Have a craving for chocolate? Try this warm chocolaty cake.

Gather Ingredients

* 4 tablespoons flour

* 4 tablespoons sugar

* 2 tablespoons cocoa

* 1 egg

* 3 tablespoons milk

* 3 tablespoons vegetable oil

* 3 tablespoons chocolate chips

* ⅛ teaspoon vanilla extract

* Your choice of topping
    - Whipped topping
    - Ice cream

Gather Equipment

Put a paper towel on your cooking area to catch spills.

* Microwave

* 1 (16 ounce) microwave-safe mug

* Measuring spoons

* 2 small bowls
  Catch spills: measure over bowl.
  Catch shells: crack egg into bowl first.

* 1 plastic knife
  Use knife to level ingredients.

* 1 kitchen fork

* 2 pot holders

Cooking Directions

Make Cake

1. **Measure** and **level** 4 tablespoons flour. **Add** to mug.

2. **Measure** and **level** 4 tablespoons sugar. **Add** to mug.

3. **Measure** and **level** 2 tablespoons cocoa. **Add** to mug.

4. **Mix** with kitchen fork.

5. **Crack** egg into small bowl. **Remove** any egg shell pieces. **Add** to mug.

6. **Mix** with kitchen fork.

7. **Measure** 3 tablespoons milk. **Add** to mug.
   Catch spills: measure milk over small bowl, then add to mug.

8. **Measure** 3 tablespoons vegetable oil. **Add** to mug.
   Catch spills: measure vegetable oil over small bowl, then add to mug.

9. **Mix** with kitchen fork.

10. **Measure** 3 tablespoons chocolate chips. **Add** to mug.

11. **Measure** ⅛ teaspoon vanilla extract. **Add** to mug.
    Catch spills: measure vanilla over small bowl, then add to mug.

12. **Mix** with kitchen fork.

13. **Microwave** 3 minutes. **Remove** from microwave with pot holders.

14. **Let** cake cool 5 minutes.

Add Toppings

1. **Add** your choice of toppings
      - 1 scoop whipped topping
      - 1 scoop ice cream

~ ENJOY!! ~

*When you finish cooking:
1. Put your ingredients and equipment away.
2. Wash and put your dishes away.
3. Wipe your cooking area clean.

Chocolate Pudding Pie

Makes 8 Pieces

An elegant dessert.

Gather Ingredients

* 1 ready-made graham cracker pie crust

* 1 (5.9 ounce) instant chocolate pudding mix

* 2½ cups milk

* Whipped topping

Gather Equipment

Put a paper towel on your cooking area to catch spills.

* 1 large mixing bowl

* 1 pie plate

* 1 liquid measuring cup

* 1 whisk

* 1 rubber spatula

* Timer

* Plastic wrap

Cooking Directions

Prepare Pie Crust

1. **Open** pie crust package.

2. **Gently** lift foil around edge of pie crust.

3. **Remove** plastic cover.

4. **Gently** press foil back down around edge of pie crust.

5. **Place** pie crust with aluminum plate into your pie plate. **Set aside.**
   This will make it easier to move your pie plate.

Make Pudding

1. **Open** (5.9 ounce) package of instant chocolate pudding mix.

2. **Pour** pudding mix into large mixing bowl.

3. **Measure** 2½ cups milk in liquid measuring cup. **Add** to pudding mix.

4. **Mix** with whisk for 2 minutes. Set timer.

Make Pie

1. **Pour** pudding into pie crust.

2. **Smooth** pudding evenly in pie crust with rubber spatula.

3. **Cover** pie with plastic wrap. **Put** in refrigerator for 1 hour or more to thicken.

Decorate Pie

1. **Top** each piece of pie with a scoop of whipped topping before serving.

~ ENJOY!! ~

*When you finish cooking:
1. Put your ingredients and equipment away.
2. Wash and put your dishes away.
3. Wipe your cooking area clean.

Chocolate Shortbread Cookies

Makes 8 Cookies

These cookies are fun to make.

Gather Ingredients

* 8 rectangular-shaped shortbread cookies

* 4 snack size chocolate bars

* Multi-color sprinkles

Gather Equipment

Put a paper towel on your cooking area to catch spills.

* Microwave

* 1 microwave-safe dinner plate

* Wax paper

* 1 kitchen knife

* 1 serving plate

* 2 Pot holders

Cooking Directions

Prepare Cookies

1. **Cover** microwave-safe dinner plate with wax paper.

2. **Put** 8 shortbread cookies on dinner plate in a circle around the edge of plate.

3. **Put** ½ piece of a snack sized chocolate bar on each cookie.

4. **Put** plate in microwave. **Microwave** 1 minute and 30 seconds.

5. **Remove** plate with pot holders.

Decorate 1 cookie at a time

1. **Spread** melted chocolate over cookie with kitchen knife.

2. **Sprinkle** chocolate with multi-color sprinkles.

3. **Finish** all 8 cookies.

4. **Put** plate in refrigerator for about 2 hours until chocolate hardens.

5. **Remove** cookies to serving plate.

~ *ENJOY!!* ~

When you finish cooking:
1. Put your ingredients and equipment away.
2. Wash and put your dishes away.
3. Wipe your cooking area clean.

Cinnamon Raisin Bread Pudding

Makes 4 Servings

You will want to make this dessert often.

Gather Ingredients

* 1 cup milk

* ¼ cup sugar plus 1 tablespoon sugar

* 2 eggs

* ½ teaspoon vanilla

* 8 slices cinnamon raisin bread

Gather Equipment

Put a paper towel on your cooking area to catch spills.

* Microwave

* 1 8x8 square microwave-safe dish

* 1 large mixing bowl

* 1 wooden spoon

* 1 whisk

* Measuring spoons

* Timer

* 1 liquid measuring cup

* ¼ dry measuring cup

* 1 small bowl Catch spills: measure over bowl. Catch shells: crack eggs into bowl first.

* 1 plastic knife Use knife to level ingredients.

* Non-stick cooking spray

* 2 pot holders

Cooking Directions

Prepare 8 x 8 microwave-safe dish

1. **Spray** 8 x 8 microwave safe dish with non-stick cooking spray. **Set aside.**

Make Pudding

1. **Measure** 1 cup milk in liquid measuring cup. **Pour** into large mixing bowl.

2. **Measure** and **level** ¼ cup sugar in dry measuring cup. **Add** to milk.

3. **Crack** 1 egg into small bowl. **Remove** any egg shell pieces. **Add** to milk.

4. **Crack** 2nd egg into small bowl. **Remove** any egg shell pieces. **Add** to milk.

5. **Measure** ½ teaspoon vanilla. **Add** to milk.
   Catch spills: measure vanilla over small bowl, then add to milk.

6. **Mix** with whisk.

7. **Tear** 8 slices cinnamon raisin bread with your fingers into small pieces.

8. **Add** bread pieces to milk. **Mix** with wooden spoon. **Wait** 3 minutes. Set timer.

9. **Mix** with wooden spoon. **Wait** 2 minutes. Set timer.

10. **Mix** with wooden spoon. **Pour** into 8x8 microwave-safe dish.

11. **Measure** and **level** 1 tablespoon sugar. **Sprinkle** over top of pudding.

Cook Bread Pudding

1. **Microwave** 7 minutes. Cook 2 minutes longer if center is not firm.

~ ENJOY!! ~

* When you finish cooking:
1. Put your ingredients and equipment away.
2. Wash and put your dishes away.
3. Wipe your cooking area clean.

Heavenly Strawberry Sauce

Makes 4 Servings

Heavenly over ice cream or a piece of pound cake!

Gather Equipment

Put a paper towel on your cooking area to catch spills.

* 1 colander

* 1 medium mixing bowl

* 1 wooden spoon

* 1 cutting board

* 1 plastic knife
  Be safe: cut with a plastic knife

* ¼ cup dry measuring cup

* Timer

Gather Ingredients

* 1 (16 ounce) basket strawberries

* ¼ cup sugar

Cooking Directions

Prepare Strawberries

1. **Put** colander in sink.

2. **Pour** strawberries into colander. **Rinse** with cold water.

3. **Cut** stems off strawberries on cutting board.
   Be safe: cut stems off with a plastic knife.

4. **Cut** each strawberry into 4 pieces. **Put** pieces into mixing bowl.

Make Sauce

1. **Measure** and **level** ¼ cup sugar in dry measuring cup. **Add** to strawberries.

2. **Mix** with wooden spoon. **Let** strawberries sit in bowl for 15 minutes. Set timer.

Serve

1. Serve over ice cream or a piece of pound cake.

~ ENJOY!! ~

FUN FACT The average strawberry has 200 seeds.

*When you finish cooking:
1. Put your ingredients and equipment away.
2. Wash and put your dishes away.
3. Wipe your cooking area clean.

Holiday Blueberry Tarts

Makes 6 Tarts

Red, white and blue; a perfect 4th of July dessert!

Gather Ingredients

* 2 (6 ounce) baskets of blueberries

* 1 package ready-made mini graham cracker pie crusts

* 2 (6 ounce) containers blueberry yogurt

* 1 (8 ounce) container whipped topping

* 6 strawberries

Gather Equipment

Put a paper towel on your cooking area to catch spills.

* 1 medium mixing bowl

* 1 small bowl
  To hold blueberries.

* 1 cookie sheet

* 1 kitchen tablespoon

* 1 cup dry measuring cup

* 1 colander

* 4 paper towels

* 1 plastic knife
  Be safe: cut with a plastic knife.

* Plastic wrap

Cooking Directions

Prepare Blueberries

1. **Cover** cookie sheet with 4 paper towels.

2. **Put** colander in sink. **Pour** blueberries into colander.

3. **Rinse** blueberries with cold water. **Pour** blueberries onto cookie sheet.

4. **Spread** blueberries over cookie sheet. **Remove** stems.

5. **Put** 24 blueberries into small bowl. **Put** in refrigerator to use later for topping.

6. **Divide** the remaining blueberries into the bottom of each mini pie crust.

7. **Set aside.**

Make Yogurt Mixture

1. **Pour** 2 (6 ounce) containers of yogurt into medium mixing bowl.

2. **Measure** 1 cup whipped topping in dry measuring cup.

3. **Add** whipped topping to yogurt. **Mix** gently with kitchen tablespoon.

4. **Spoon** yogurt mixture over blueberries in the 6 pie crusts.

5. **Cover** with plastic wrap.

6. **Put** in refrigerator for at least 1 hour.

Decorate Tarts

1. **Top** each tart before serving with:
   - 1 small scoop of whipped topping
   - 4 blueberries from small bowl set aside in refrigerator
   - 1 strawberry
     Rinse strawberry with water. **Cut** stem off with plastic knife. **Put** strawberry on top of tart.

~ ENJOY!! ~

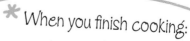

*When you finish cooking:
1. Put your ingredients and equipment away.
2. Wash and put your dishes away.
3. Wipe your cooking area clean.

103

Jello

Makes 4 Servings

Any flavor jello you like can be used in this recipe.

Gather Ingredients

* 1 (3 ounce) package Jello

* 2 cups water

Gather Equipment

Put a paper towel on your cooking area to catch spills.

* Microwave

* 1 medium mixing bowl

* 1 liquid measuring cup

* 1 kitchen tablespoon

* 2 pot holders

Cooking Directions

Make Jello

1. **Open** (3 ounce) package of jello. **Pour** into medium mixing bowl. **Set aside.**

2. **Measure** 1 cup of water in liquid measuring cup.

3. **Microwave** water for 2 minutes. **Remove** from microwave with pot holders.

4. **Add** hot water to jello.

5. **Stir** with kitchen tablespoon until jello is dissolved.
   Look down to the bottom to be sure *all* the jello is dissolved.

6. **Measure** 1 cup cold water in liquid measuring cup. **Add** cold water to jello.

7. **Stir** with kitchen tablespoon.

Let Jello Firm

1. **Put** jello in refrigerator for at least 4 hours to firm.

When you finish cooking:
1. Put your ingredients and equipment away.
2. Wash and put your dishes away.
3. Wipe your cooking area clean.

Key Lime Pie

Makes 6 Servings

A refreshing pie for a summer day.

Gather Ingredients

* 1 ready-made graham cracker pie crust

* 1 (14 ounce) can sweetened condensed milk

* ½ pint of heavy cream

* 1 (6 ounce) can frozen limeade concentrate do not thaw

* Whipped topping

Gather Equipment

Put a paper towel on your cooking area to catch spills.

* Electric mixer

* 1 large mixing bowl

* 1 pie plate

* 1 kitchen tablespoon

* 1 rubber spatula

* Timer

* Plastic wrap

Cooking Directions

Prepare Pie Crust

1. **Open** pie crust package.

2. **Gently** lift foil around edge of pie crust.

3. **Remove** plastic cover.

4. **Gently** press foil back down around edge of pie crust.

5. **Place** pie crust with aluminum plate into your pie plate. **Set aside.**
   This will make it easier to move your pie plate.

Make Filling

1. **Open** (14 ounce) sweetened condensed milk. **Pour** into large mixing bowl.

2. **Open** ½ pint heavy cream. **Add** to condensed milk.

3. **Open** (6 ounce) limeade can. **Add** to condensed milk.

4. **Beat** with electric mixer until fluffy and soft peaks form. About 3 minutes.
   Set timer.

Make Pie

1. **Pour** filling into pie crust.

2. **Smooth** filling evenly in pie crust with rubber spatula.

3. **Cover** pie with plastic wrap. **Put** in refrigerator for at least 4 hours to firm.

Decorate Pie

1. **Top** each piece of pie with a scoop of whipped topping before serving.

~ ENJOY!! ~

*When you finish cooking:
1. Put your ingredients and equipment away.
2. Wash and put your dishes away.
3. Wipe your cooking area clean.

Mandarin Orange Jello

Makes 4 Servings

Hmmm, Hmmm Good! Everyone will ask you how to make this.

Gather Ingredients

* 1 (11 ounce) can mandarin oranges

* 1 pint vanilla ice cream

* 2 (3 ounce) packages orange jello

Gather Equipment

Put a paper towel on your cooking area to catch spills.

* Microwave

* 8x8 square microwave-safe dish

* 2 cup liquid measuring cup

* 1 colander

* 1 kitchen tablespoon

* 1 can opener

* Plastic wrap

* 2 pot holders

Cooking Directions

Prepare Mandarin Oranges

1. **Put** colander in sink.

2. **Open** (11 ounce) mandarin oranges can. **Pour** oranges into colander.

3. **Let** juice drain. **Set aside.**

Make Jello

1. **Open** 2 (3 ounce) packages of orange jello.

2. **Pour** jello into 8x8 microwave-safe dish. **Set aside.**

3. **Measure** 2 cups of water in 2-cup liquid measuring cup.

4. **Microwave** water 3 minutes. **Remove** from microwave with pot holders.

5. **Add** hot water to jello.

6. **Stir** with kitchen tablespoon until jello is dissolved.
   Look down to the bottom to be sure *all* the jello is dissolved.

7. **Add** 1 pint vanilla ice cream to jello.

8. **Stir** with kitchen tablespoon until ice cream melts.

9. **Add** drained mandarin oranges to jello. **Stir** with kitchen tablespoon.

10. **Cover** with plastic wrap.

Let Jello Firm

1. **Put** jello in refrigerator for at least 4 hours to firm.

~ ENJOY!! ~

*When you finish cooking:
1. Put your ingredients and equipment away.
2. Wash and put your dishes away.
3. Wipe your cooking area clean.

Rainbow Vanilla Pudding

Makes 4 Servings

Rainbow Sprinkles will surprise everyone when you serve this dessert.

Gather Ingredients

* 1 (3.4 ounce) instant vanilla pudding mix
* 2 cups milk
* 1½ tablespoons rainbow sprinkles
* Whipped topping

Gather Equipment

Put a paper towel on your cooking area to catch spills.

* 1 large mixing bowl
* 1 liquid measuring cup
* Measuring spoons
* 1 whisk
* 1 kitchen tablespoon
* Timer
* 4 small serving bowls

Cooking Directions

Make Pudding

1. **Open** (3.4 ounce) package of instant vanilla pudding.

2. **Pour** into large mixing bowl.

3. **Measure** 2 cups milk in liquid measuring cup. **Add** to pudding.

4. **Mix** with whisk for 2 minutes. Set timer.

5. **Measure** and **level** 1½ tablespoons rainbow sprinkles.

6. **Add** sprinkles to pudding.

7. **Mix** gently with whisk.

8. **Wait** 5 minutes before serving. Set timer.

Decorate Pudding

1. **Spoon** pudding into 4 small serving bowls.

2. **Top** each pudding with 1 scoop of whipped topping.

3. **Sprinkle** rainbow sprinkles on top of whipped topping.

~ ENJOY!! ~

* When you finish cooking:
1. Put your ingredients and equipment away.
2. Wash and put your dishes away.
3. Wipe your cooking area clean.

St. Patty's Banana Cream Pudding
Makes 4 Servings

Celebrate St. Patrick's Day, March 17th, with this dessert.

Gather Ingredients

* 1 (3.4 ounce) instant banana cream pudding mix

* 2 cups milk

* Green food coloring

* Whipped topping

* Green sprinkles

Gather Equipment

Put a paper towel on your cooking area to catch spills.

* 1 large mixing bowl

* 1 liquid measuring cup

* 1 whisk

* 1 kitchen tablespoon

* Timer

* 4 small serving bowls

Cooking Directions

Make Pudding

1. **Open** (3.4 ounce) package of instant banana cream pudding mix.

2. **Pour** into large mixing bowl.

3. **Measure** 2 cups milk in liquid measuring cup. **Add** to pudding.

4. **Mix** with whisk for 2 minutes. Set timer.

5. **Add** 4 drops of green food coloring.

6. **Mix** with whisk.

7. **Wait** 5 minutes before serving. Set timer.

Decorate Pudding

1. **Spoon** pudding into 4 small serving bowls

2. **Top** each pudding with 1 scoop of whipped topping.

3. **Sprinkle** green sprinkles on top of whipped topping.

 ~ ENJOY!! ~

*When you finish cooking:
1. Put your ingredients and equipment away.
2. Wash and put your dishes away.
3. Wipe your cooking area clean.

Favorite
Drink & Snack
Recipes

dessert entre

_____
_____
_____
_____
_____
_____
_____
_____
_____
_____
_____

February is National Food Snack Month!!

FUN FACT Strawberries are the only fruit with seeds on the outside.

FUN FACT October is National Pizza Month!

~ DRINKS & SNACKS ~

*A little more challenging

Banana Strawberry Smoothie

Makes 1 Smoothie

*Ohooo, so good!
And healthy too!*

Gather Equipment

Put a paper towel on your cooking area to catch spills

* Electric blender

* 1 cutting board

* 1 liquid measuring cup

* 1 cup dry measuring cup

* 1 plastic knife
  Be safe: cut with a plastic knife.

* 1 large mug

Gather Ingredients

* ¼ cup orange juice

* 7 fresh strawberries

* 1 banana

* 1 cup ice cubes

Cooking Directions

1. **Measure** ¼ cup orange juice in liquid measuring cup. **Pour** into blender.

2. **Put** 7 fresh strawberries in your hand. **Rinse** with cold water in sink.

3. **Cut** stems off strawberries on cutting board.
   Be safe: cut strawberry stems off with a plastic knife.

4. **Add** strawberries to blender.

5. **Peel** 1 banana. **Cut** banana in half. **Add** to blender.
   Be safe: cut banana with a plastic knife.

6. **Measure** 1 cup ice in dry measuring cup. **Add** to blender.

Mix Smoothie

1. **Put** cover on blender. **Keep** one hand on blender cover.

2. **Mix** for 30 seconds. Count to 30

3. **Pour** into large mug.

~ ENJOY!! ~

✻ When you finish cooking:
1. Put your ingredients and equipment away.
2. Wash and put your dishes away.
3. Wipe your cooking area clean.

Chocolate Milk Shake

Makes 1 Shake

An old time favorite!

Gather Equipment

Put a paper towel on your cooking area to catch spills.

* Electric blender

* 1 kitchen tablespoon

* 1 ice cream scoop

* 1 liquid measuring cup

* 1 large mug

* 1 straw

Gather Ingredients

* 1 cup milk

* 3 large scoops chocolate ice cream

* 4 tablespoons chocolate syrup

Cooking Directions

Make Shake

1. **Measure** 1 cup milk in liquid measuring cup. **Pour** into blender.

2. **Add** 3 large scoops of chocolate ice cream to blender.

3. **Add** 4 kitchen tablespoons chocolate syrup to blender.
   Catch spills: measure chocolate syrup over blender.

Mix Shake

1. **Put** cover on blender. **Keep** one hand on blender cover.

2. **Mix** for 30 seconds. Count to 30

3. **Pour** into large mug.

4. **Add** straw.

~ ENJOY!! ~

* When you finish cooking:
1. Put your ingredients and equipment away.
2. Wash and put your dishes away.
3. Wipe your cooking area clean.

Cool Orange Julius

Makes 1 Smoothie

Cool and refreshing after a swim in the pool.

Gather Ingredients

* 1 (6 ounce) can frozen orange juice
* 1 cup milk
* 1 cup water
* ¼ cup sugar
* 1 teaspoon vanilla
* 8 ice cubes

Gather Equipment

Put a paper towel on your cooking area to catch spills.

* Electric blender
* ¼ dry measuring cup
* 1 liquid measuring cup
* Measuring spoons
* 1 small bowl
  Catch spills: measure over bowl.
* 1 plastic knife
  Use to level ingredients.
* 1 large mug
* 1 small mixing bowl
  To hold ice cubes.

Cooking Directions

Make Smoothie

1. **Pour** (6 ounce) can frozen orange juice into blender.

2. **Measure** 1 cup of milk in liquid measuring cup. **Add** to blender.

3. **Measure** 1 cup water in liquid measuring cup. **Add** to blender.

4. **Measure** and **level** ¼ cup sugar in dry measuring cup. **Add** to blender.

5. **Measure** 1 teaspoon vanilla. **Add** to blender.
   Catch spills: measure vanilla over small bowl, then add to blender.

Mix Smoothie

1. **Put** blender cover on. **Keep** one hand on blender cover.

2. **Mix** for 30 seconds. Count to 30

3. **Put** 8 ice cubes from freezer into small bowl.

4. **Add** ice cubes to blender.

5. **Put** blender cover on. **Keep** one hand on blender cover.

6. **Mix** for 30 seconds. Count to 30

7. **Pour** into large mug.

~ ENJOY!! ~

* When you finish cooking:
1. Put your ingredients and equipment away.
2. Wash and put your dishes away.
3. Wipe your cooking area clean.

Easy Cheesy Nachos

Makes 1 Serving

Top your cheese nachos with sour cream and salsa to make "supreme nachos".

Gather Equipment

Put a paper towel on your cooking area to catch spills.

* Microwave

* microwave-safe plate

* ¼ dry measuring cup

* 2 pot holders

Gather Ingredients

* 16 large tortilla chips

* ¼ cup shredded Jack cheese

* ¼ cup shredded Cheddar cheese

* Your choice of toppings
    - 1 tablespoon sour cream
    - 1 tablespoon salsa

Cooking Directions

Make Nachos

1. **Spread** 16 tortilla chips on microwave-safe plate.

2. **Measure** ¼ cup shredded Jack cheese in dry measuring cup.

3. **Sprinkle** Jack cheese over tortilla chips.

4. **Measure** ¼ cup shredded Cheddar cheese in dry measuring cup.

5. **Sprinkle** Cheddar cheese over tortilla chips.

6. **Microwave** at 50% power for 30 seconds.
   Hit the **power button** until it reads 5. Then press in 30 seconds.

7. **Remove** nachos from microwave with pot holders.

Add Toppings

1. **Add** your choice of toppings
   - 1 tablespoon sour cream
   - 1 tablespoon salsa

~ ENJOY!! ~

***When you finish cooking:**
1. Put your ingredients and equipment away.
2. Wash and put your dishes away.
3. Wipe your cooking area clean.

Easy Hummus

Makes: 1½ Cups

Easy and delicious!!

Gather Ingredients

* 1 (15 ounce) can garbanzo beans

* ½ cup sun-dried tomato salad dressing

* 1 teaspoon minced garlic
  Garlic from a jar is easier to use.

* 1 bag baked pita chips

Gather Equipment

Put a paper towel on your cooking area to catch spills.

* Electric blender

* Colander

* Can opener

* 1 wooden spoon

* Measuring spoons

* 1 liquid measuring cup

* 1 small serving bowl

* 1 large serving bowl

Cooking Directions

Combine Hummus Ingredients

1. **Put** colander in sink.

2. **Open** (15 ounce) can garbanzo beans.

3. **Pour** beans into colander.

4. **Rinse** beans under cold water in sink. **Let** water drain out.

5. **Pour** beans into electric blender.

6. **Measure** ½ cup sun-dried tomato dressing in liquid measuring cup.

7. **Pour** dressing into electric blender.

8. **Measure** 1 teaspoon minced garlic. **Add** to electric blender.

Mix Hummus

1. **Put** cover on blender. **Keep** one hand on blender cover.

2. **Mix** for 30 seconds. Count to 30.

Serve Hummus and Chips

1. **Empty** hummus into small serving bowl.

2. **Pour** chips into large serving bowl.

~ ENJOY!! ~

* When you finish cooking:
1. Put your ingredients and equipment away.
2. Wash and put your dishes away.
3. Wipe your cooking area clean.

Fishy Trail Mix

Makes 5 Cups

A great snack for school, on the trail, or watching a movie.

Gather Ingredients

- 1 cup fish-shaped Cheddar crackers
- 1 cup round honey-nut toasted oat cereal
- 1 cup pretzels sticks
- 1 cup raisins
- 1 cup peanuts

Gather Equipment

Put a paper towel on your cooking area to catch spills.

- 1 large mixing bowl
- 1 cup dry measuring cup
- 1 wooden spoon
- 4 sandwich storage bags

Cooking Directions

Make Trail Mix

1. **Measure** 1 cup fish-shaped Cheddar crackers in dry measuring cup.

2. **Pour** into large mixing bowl.

3. **Measure** 1 cup honey-nut oat cereal in dry measuring cup.

4. **Add** to crackers.

5. **Measure** 1 cup of pretzel sticks in dry measuring cup.

6. **Break** pretzel sticks in half. **Add** pretzels to crackers.

7. **Measure** 1 cup raisins in dry measuring cup.

8. **Add** to crackers.

9. **Measure** 1 cup peanuts in dry measuring cup.

10. **Add** to crackers.

11. **Mix** with wooden spoon.

Fill Storage Bags

1. **Divide** into 4 storage bags using 1 cup dry measuring cup.

~ ENJOY!! ~

*When you finish cooking:
1. Put your ingredients and equipment away.
2. Wash and put your dishes away.
3. Wipe your cooking area clean.

Fresh Veggie Platter

Makes 1 Platter

A tasty crowd pleaser anytime!

Gather Ingredients

* 1 (16 ounce) container sour cream

* 1 package dry vegetable soup mix

* 1 (10 ounce) container cherry tomatoes

* 1 container celery sticks

* 1 bag mini carrots

Gather Equipment

Put a paper towel on your cooking area to catch spills.

* 1 medium mixing bowl

* 1 wooden spoon

* 1 colander

* 1 serving platter

Cooking Directions

Make Dip

1. **Empty** (16 ounce) container of sour cream into medium mixing bowl.

2. **Add** dry vegetable soup mix package to sour cream.

3. Mix with wooden spoon.
   Be sure to stir all the way down to the bottom of the bowl and up the sides.

4. **Put** dish in middle of serving platter.

Prepare Veggie Platter

1. **Put** colander in sink.

2. **Empty** cherry tomatoes into colander. **Rinse** with cold water.

3. **Put** cherry tomatoes in 1 section of serving platter.

4. **Put** celery sticks in 2nd section of serving platter.

5. **Put** mini carrots in 3rd section of serving platter.

~ ENJOY!! ~

* When you finish cooking:
1. Put your ingredients and equipment away.
2. Wash and put your dishes away.
3. Wipe your cooking area clean.

Go Green & Shake

Makes 1 Shake

A fun treat for St. Patrick's Day, March 17th.

Gather Equipment

Put a paper towel on your cooking area to catch spills.

* Electric blender

* 1 ice cream scoop

* 1 liquid measuring cup

* 1 kitchen tablespoon

* 1 large mug

* 1 straw

Gather Ingredients

* 1 cup milk

* 3 large scoops vanilla ice cream

* Green food coloring

* 1 tablespoon whipped topping

* Green sprinkles

Cooking Directions

Make Shake

1. **Measure** 1 cup milk in liquid measuring cup. **Pour** into blender.

2. **Add** 3 large scoops of vanilla ice cream to blender.

3. **Add** 3 drops of green food coloring to blender.

Mix Shake

1. **Put** cover on blender. Keep one hand on blender cover.

2. **Mix** for 30 seconds. Count to 30

3. **Pour** into large mug.

Decorate Shake

1. **Scoop** 1 tablespoon of whipped topping on top of shake.

2. **Sprinkle** green sprinkles on top of whipped topping.

3. **Add** straw.

~ ENJOY!! ~

*When you finish cooking:
1. Put your ingredients and equipment away.
2. Wash and put your dishes away.
3. Wipe your cooking area clean.

Nutty Trail Mix

Makes 5 Cups

A yummy trail mix when you need a little extra energy.

Gather Equipment

Put a paper towel on your cooking area to catch spills.

* 1 large mixing bowl

* Dry measuring cups

* 1 wooden spoon

* 4 sandwich storage bags

Gather Ingredients

* 1½ cups lightly salted mixed nuts

* 1 cup M&M's

* 1 cup raisins

Cooking Directions

Make Trail Mix

1. **Measure** 1½ cups mixed nuts in dry measuring cups.

2. **Pour** into large mixing bowl.

3. **Measure** 1 cup M&M's in dry measuring cup.

4. **Add** to mixed nuts.

5. **Measure** 1 cup raisins in dry measuring cup.

6. **Add** to mixed nuts.

7. **Mix** with wooden spoon.

Fill Storage Bags

1. **Divide** into 4 storage bags using 1 cup dry measuring cup.

~ ENJOY!! ~

* When you finish cooking:

1. Put your ingredients and equipment away.
2. Wash and put your dishes away.
3. Wipe your cooking area clean.

Orange Shake

Makes 1 Shake

A refreshing frothy orange shake.

Gather Equipment

Put a paper towel on your cooking area to catch spills.

* Electric blender

* 1 liquid measuring cup

* 1 ice cream scoop

* 1 large mug

* 1 straw

Gather Ingredients

* 1 cup orange juice

* 3 large scoops vanilla ice cream

Cooking Directions

Make Shake

1. **Measure** 1 cup orange juice in liquid measuring cup. **Pour** into blender.

2. **Add** 3 large scoops of vanilla ice cream to blender.

Mix Shake

1. **Put** blender cover on. **Keep** one hand on blender cover.

2. **Mix** for 30 seconds. Count to 30

3. **Pour** into large mug. **Add** straw.

~ ENJOY!! ~

FUN FACT   There are 600 types of oranges in the world.

* When you finish cooking:
1. Put your ingredients and equipment away.
2. Wash and put your dishes away.
3. Wipe your cooking area clean.

Quick Pizza Snack

Makes 1 Pizza Snack

Don't wait for delivery. Make your own quick pizza snack.

Gather Equipment

Put a paper towel on your cooking area to catch spills.

* Microwave and toaster

* Measuring spoons

* 1 plastic knife
  Be safe: cut with a plastic knife.

* 2 pot holders

* 1 serving plate

Gather Ingredients

* 1 mini plain bagel
     or
  1 English muffin

* 2 tablespoons pizza sauce

* 2 tablespoons shredded pizza cheese

136

Cooking Directions

Toast Bagel or English Muffin

1. **Cut** bagel or English muffin in half. **Put** bagel or English muffin into toaster.
Be safe: cut bagel or English muffin with a plastic knife.

2. **Push** toaster on.

3. **Put** toasted bagel or English muffin halves on serving plate side-by-side.

Add Pizza Toppings

1. **Spread** each half with 1 tablespoon of pizza sauce.

2. **Sprinkle** 1 tablespoon of shredded pizza cheese over pizza sauce.

Cook Pizza

1. **Microwave** pizza 20 seconds to melt cheese.

2. **Remove** pizza from microwave with pot holders.

3. **Let** pizza cool before eating.

~ ENJOY!! ~

* When you finish cooking:
1. Put your ingredients and equipment away.
2. Wash and put your dishes away.
3. Wipe your cooking area clean.

Root Beer Float

Makes 1 Float

Nothing screams summer like a root beer float.

Gather Ingredients

* 2 large scoops vanilla ice cream

* 1 can root beer

Gather Equipment

Put a paper towel on your cooking area to catch spills.

* 1 large mug

* 1 ice cream scoop

* 1 straw

* 1 spoon

Cooking Directions

Make Float

1. **Put** 2 large scoops of vanilla ice cream into mug.

2. **Pour** root beer "slowly" into mug.

3. **Add** straw and spoon.

~ ENJOY!! ~

FUN FACT The Root Beer Float was first called the "Brown Cow".

*When you finish cooking:
1. Put your ingredients and equipment away.
2. Wash and put your dishes away.
3. Wipe your cooking area clean.

139

Salsa Onion Dip and Chips

Makes 2 Cups of Dip

Everyone's party favorite.

Gather Ingredients

* 1 (16 ounce) container sour cream

* 1 envelope dry onion soup mix

* ½ cup salsa

* 1 bag potato chips

Gather Equipment

Put a paper towel on your cooking area to catch spills.

* 1 medium serving bowl

* 1 wooden spoon

* ½ cup dry measuring cup

* 1 serving platter

Cooking Directions

Make Dip

1. **Empty** (16 ounce) container of sour cream into medium serving bowl.

2. **Add** dry onion soup mix to sour cream.

3. **Measure** ½ cup salsa in dry measuring cup. **Add** to sour cream.

4. **Mix** with wooden spoon.
   Be sure to stir all the way down to the bottom of the bowl and up the sides.

5. **Put** dip in the middle of the serving platter.

Prepare Platter

1. **Add** potato chips around bowl.

~ ENJOY!! ~

FUN FACT The largest onion ever grown weighed 10 pounds and 14 ounces.

* When you finish cooking:
1. Put your ingredients and equipment away.
2. Wash and put your dishes away.
3. Wipe your cooking area clean.

Salsa Snack

Makes 25 or more

A great snack while watching a movie.

Gather Ingredients

* 1 box of plain crackers

* 1 (6 ounce) container cream cheese spread

* 1 (16 ounce) container chunky salsa

Gather Equipment

Put a paper towel on your cooking area to catch spills.

* 1 kitchen knife

* 1 kitchen fork

* 1 serving platter

Cooking Directions

Make Snack

1. **Spread** 1 cracker with cream cheese.

2. **Put** a small kitchen fork-full of salsa on top of cream cheese.

3. **Eat** as you go or . . . **make** a platter full to share.

~ ENJOY!! ~

* When you finish cooking:
1. Put your ingredients and equipment away.
2. Wash and put your dishes away.
3. Wipe your cooking area clean.

S'mores

Makes 1 S'more

August 10th is National S'mores Day! Awesome!

Gather Equipment

Put a paper towel on your cooking area to catch spills.

* Microwave

* 1 microwave-safe plate

Gather Ingredients

* 1 whole graham cracker

* ½ plain chocolate bar

* 1 large marshmallow

Cooking Directions

Make S'more

1. **Break** graham cracker in half. You should have 2 squares.

2. **Place** 1 graham cracker square on microwave-safe plate.

3. **Put** ½ chocolate bar on graham cracker.

4. **Put** 1 large marshmallow on top of chocolate.

Cook S'more

1. **Microwave** 15 seconds.

2. **Remove** from microwave. **Cover** with 2nd graham cracker square.

3. **Eat** like a sandwich.

~ ENJOY!! ~

*When you finish cooking:
1. Put your ingredients and equipment away.
2. Wash and put your dishes away.
3. Wipe your cooking area clean.

Toothpick Munchies

Makes 35 Snacks

A wonderful appetizer for a barbeque.

Gather Ingredients

* 1 bunch green grapes

* ½ pound thinly sliced salami

* 1 (8 ounce) package Cheddar cheese cubes

Gather Equipment

Put a paper towel on your cooking area to catch spills.

* About 35 toothpicks

* 1 colander

* 1 cookie sheet

* 2 paper towels

* 1 serving platter

Cooking Directions

Prepare Fruit

1. **Cover** cookie sheet with 2 paper towels.

2. **Put** colander in sink.

3. **Empty** grapes into colander. **Rinse** with cold water.

4. **Empty** grapes onto cookie sheet.

Prepare Salami & Cheese

1. **Open** packages of salami and Cheddar cheese cubes.

Make Toothpick Munchies

1. **Poke** 1 grape onto toothpick.

2. **Fold** salami in half and in half again. **Push** onto toothpick with grape.

3. **Slide** 1 cheddar cheese cube onto toothpick with salami and grape.

4. **Put** toothpick nibbles on serving platter as you make them.

5. **Continue** making until you run out of cheese cubes.

Leftovers

1. **Put** leftover grapes in the middle of the serving platter.

2. **Fold** leftover salami in half and in half again. **Push** onto a toothpick.

3. **Add** folded salami to serving platter.

~ ENJOY!! ~

When you finish cooking:
1. Put your ingredients and equipment away.
2. Wash and put your dishes away.
3. Wipe your cooking area clean.

Favorite
Vegetable
Recipes

_____
_____
_____
_____
_____

_____
_____
_____
_____
_____
_____

Power your diet with vegetables

FUN FACT In October 1995, the potato became the first vegetable grown in space.

FUN FACT A rabbit eating one carrot is like us eating over 20 carrots.

~ VEGETABLES ~

*A little more challenging

Baked Potato

Makes 1 Baked Potato

Add your favorite toppings and make this potato just the way you like it.

Gather Ingredients

* 1 large Idaho baking potato

* Your choice of toppings
    - ½ tablespoon butter
    - ½ tablespoon sour cream
    - Salt and pepper shakers
    - ½ teaspoon dried chives
    - 1 tablespoon shredded Cheddar cheese

Gather Equipment

Put a paper towel on your cooking area to catch spills.

* Microwave

* 1 paper towel

* 1 sponge

* 1 kitchen fork

* 1 plastic knife
  Be safe: cut with a plastic knife.

* Measuring spoons

* 1 serving plate

* 2 pot holders

Cooking Directions

Cook Potato

1. **Lay** 1 paper towel in microwave.

2. **Scrub** potato clean with sponge under cold water in sink.

3. **Stab** potato 3 times with kitchen fork.

4. **Put** potato on the paper towel in microwave.

5. **Microwave** for 15 minutes.

6. **Check** if potato is done when microwave timer goes off.
    - **Insert** kitchen fork into potato. It should be soft.
    - If not soft, **microwave** 1 minute more.

7. **Remove** potato from microwave with pot holders.

8. **Put** potato on serving plate.

9. **Cut** potato in half the long way.
   Be safe: cut potato with a plastic knife.

10. **Mash** up the insides with kitchen fork.

Add Toppings

1. **Add** your choice of toppings
    - ½ tablespoon butter
    - ½ tablespoon sour cream
    - 4 shakes of salt and pepper
    - ½ teaspoon dried chives
    - 1 tablespoon shredded Cheddar cheese

~ ENJOY!! ~

* When you finish cooking:
1. Put your ingredients and equipment away.
2. Wash and put your dishes away.
3. Wipe your cooking area clean.

Corn on the Cob

Makes 1 Ear of Corn

Here's a quick way to cook one ear of corn.

Gather Equipment

Put a paper towel on your cooking area to catch spills.

* Microwave

* 1 paper towel

* 1 kitchen towel

* Timer

* 1 serving plate

* 2 pot holders

Gather Ingredients

* 1 ear of corn with husks and silk

* Your choice of toppings
  - Butter
  - Salt

Cooking Directions

Prepare Microwave

1. **Wet** paper towel with cold water in kitchen sink.

2. **Squeeze** water out of paper towel.

3. **Flatten** wet paper towel and **lay** it down flat in the microwave.

Cook Corn *(Do Not Remove Husks and Silk from Corn)*

1. **Put** corn on wet paper towel. **Microwave** 2 minutes.

2. **Turn** corn over. **Microwave** 2 minutes.

3. **Remove** corn from microwave with pot holders.

4. **Wrap** corn in kitchen towel. **Leave** corn in towel for 5 minutes. Set timer.

Serve Corn

1. **Remove** corn husks and silk over kitchen trash can.

2. **Put** corn on serving plate.

Add Toppings

1. **Add** your choice of toppings
   - 1 tablespoon butter
   - Sprinkle with salt

~ ENJOY!! ~

* When you finish cooking:
1. Put your ingredients and equipment away.
2. Wash and put your dishes away.
3. Wipe your cooking area clean.

Fresh Mini Carrots

Makes 1 Serving

Tasty, healthy!

Gather Ingredients

* 1 cup fresh mini carrots

* 1 tablespoon water

Gather Equipment

Put a paper towel on your cooking area to catch spills.

* Microwave

* 1 medium microwave-safe bowl

* Measuring spoons

* 1 cup dry measuring cup

* Timer

* Plastic wrap

* 2 pot holders

Cooking Directions

Prepare Carrots

1. **Measure** 1 cup of mini carrots in dry measuring cup.

2. **Empty** carrots into medium microwave-safe bowl.

3. **Measure** 2 tablespoons water. **Add** to carrots.

4. **Cover** bowl with plastic wrap.

Cook Carrots

1. **Microwave** 3 minutes. **Remove** bowl from microwave with pot holders.

2. **Wait** 5 minutes before removing plastic wrap. Set timer.

3. **Remove** plastic wrap carefully. Steam will be hot.

* When you finish cooking:
1. Put your ingredients and equipment away.
2. Wash and put your dishes away.
3. Wipe your cooking area clean.

Red Bliss Garlic Mash

Makes 4 Servings

A new twist on mashed potatoes.

Gather Ingredients

* 8 small red potatoes

* ¼ cup milk

* 1 teaspoon minced garlic
  Garlic from a jar is easier to use.

* 1 tablespoon margarine

* Salt and pepper shakers

* 1 tablespoon dried chives

Gather Equipment

Put a paper towel on your cooking area to catch spills.

* Microwave

* 1 large microwave-safe plate

* Sponge

* Measuring spoons

* 1 liquid measuring cup

* 1 kitchen fork

* 1 medium mixing bowl

* 1 potato masher

* 1 wooden spoon

* Wax paper

* 2 pot holders

Cooking Directions

Cook Potatoes

1. **Scrub** 8 small red potatoes clean with sponge under cold water in sink.

2. **Stab** each potato twice with kitchen fork.

3. **Place** potatoes on large microwave-safe plate. **Microwave** 7 minutes.

Make Sauce *"while potatoes cook"*

1. **Measure** ¼ cup milk in liquid measuring cup.

2. **Measure** 1 teaspoon garlic. **Add** to milk.

3. **Measure** and level 1 tablespoon margarine. **Add** to milk.

4. **Add** 2 dashes of salt and pepper to milk.

5. **Mix** with kitchen fork. **Cover** with a piece of wax paper. **Set** aside.

Mix Potatoes and Sauce

1. **Check** if potatoes are done when microwave timer goes off.
    - **Insert** kitchen fork into potato. It should be soft.
    - If not soft, **microwave** 1 minute more.

2. **Remove** potatoes from microwave with pot holders.

3. **Empty** potatoes in medium mixing bowl. **Leave** skins on.

4. **Microwave** sauce 30 seconds. **Pour** sauce over potatoes.

5. **Mash** potatoes with potato masher. Potatoes will be chunky.

6. **Measure** 1 tablespoon dried chives. **Add** to potatoes. **Mix** with wooden spoon.

~ ENJOY!! ~

* When you finish cooking:
1. Put your ingredients and equipment away.
2. Wash and put your dishes away.
3. Wipe your cooking area clean.

Sweet Peas

Makes 1 Serving

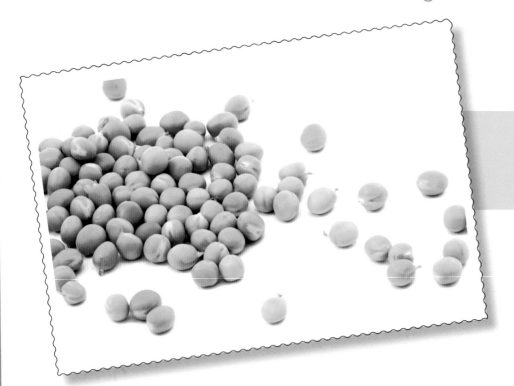

Peas please!

Gather Ingredients

* 1 cup frozen peas

* ½ tablespoon water

* ½ teaspoon margarine

Gather Equipment

Put a paper towel on your cooking area to catch spills.

* Microwave

* 1 liquid measuring cup

* Wax paper

* Measuring spoons

* 1 kitchen teaspoon

* 1 plastic knife

* 2 pot holders

Cooking Directions

Prepare Peas

1. **Measure** 1 cup peas in liquid measuring cup.

2. **Measure** 1 tablespoon water. **Pour** over peas.

3. **Cover** peas with a piece of wax paper.

Cook Peas

1. **Microwave** peas 1 minute and 30 seconds.

2. **Remove** peas from microwave with pot holders.

3. **Measure** and **level** ½ teaspoon margarine. **Add** to peas.

4. **Mix** with kitchen teaspoon.

~ ENJOY!! ~

* When you finish cooking:
1. Put your ingredients and equipment away.
2. Wash and put your dishes away.
3. Wipe your cooking area clean.

~ About the Author ~

Beverly Worth Palomba is originally from Massachusetts where she worked in the computer industry as a program manager for a well-known computer company. She moved from New England and has resided in the San Francisco Bay area for the past 25 years. She has a husband (Dick), daughter (Gina) and a kitty named Kiwi.

When she moved to California, Bev turned to her real love—education. She has been a teacher from PK through high school for more than 20 years. In the past ten years she has worked exclusively in Special Education. She created a life skills cooking class four years ago at the local high school geared to the needs and abilities of her students. In addition she provides cooking workshops at local community centers. From this curriculum has come her first book, *Special Day Cooking*, a life skills cookbook which uses a unique instructional method that people with developmental challenges have responded to and enjoyed. This book has become a labor of love.